Sangha of Two

For Karen
Best wishes!

To order additional copies, please contact us.
BookSurge, LLC
www.booksurge.com
1-866-308-6235
orders@booksurge.com

HOLLY MORRIS
BENNET

SANGHA of TWO
Eastern Thought, Western Process, Modern Seekers

2006

Sangha of Two

CONTENTS

ACKNOWLEDGEMENTS

This book is a testament to the love and energy of many people. To my parents, John and Barbara Morris, who gave me such a wonderful start in the world and developed my mind and my determination. To my clients who allowed me the privilege of being in their lives in this most intimate way and gave me so many great experiences as a coach. I thank them for their permission to use our work together. To my coaches over the last five years who gave me the other material for this book. By taking me on as a client and giving me remarkable coaching experiences each of you contributed something necessary and beautiful to my becoming the author of my life and of this book. To Grace, Ted and Flinn who led me to all the people and things I needed to complete this book. To Daia Gerson, Ann Bennet and Jon Waterman for thoughtfully engaging with the manuscript in the editing process. To my daughter, Olivia, whose toddlerhood co-existed with this book; you forced me to focus and write whenever, wherever—thank you. And finally, to my husband, Joseph, who has given me patience and support equaled only by my parents. You gave me room to grow and even when I threatened to become a weed, you held me like a hothouse flower. Enjoy this, the first of many blooms.

FOREWORD

*S*angha of Two: Eastern Thought, Western Process, Modern Seekers shows us how to merge the wisdom of Buddhism with the vibrancy of coaching and claim the best of both.

Coaching has been very successful in helping people build purposeful, value-driven, intentional lives and in helping them live beyond their jobs and daily lives and into their dreams. In the early days of coaching there was a concerted effort to keep the coaching model and its process as separate as possible from religion and psychology so as to avoid being aligned with specifically charged paradigms. But because the focus of coaching is the whole life, inquiries into personal growth, health and well being could not be made without bringing attention to the clients' spiritual, intellectual, emotional and psychological aspects.

Enter Holly Morris Bennet and her wonderful book bringing together the coaching model with one of the world's primary spiritual models. Although not a Buddhist myself, I have studied many of the eastern religions and philosophies in my personal growth process, and I am delighted to see through Holly Morris Bennet's experiences as a coach and a client how elegantly the models of co-active coaching and Buddhism fit together. In a remarkably vulnerable and entertaining way she brings us into the core concepts of both models and seamlessly shows us how to use each of them to expand the other. Whatever philosophy or religion you follow, there is value for you in this book. If you're a coach, you'll be a better coach; if you're not a coach, you will see what you can build in your life through coaching.

I believe our culture is at a crossroads where we must choose conscious evolution if we are to survive. Further, I believe that evolution will arise from our merging of successful models for human thought and behavior and discarding models that do not produce more of what people truly need—intimacy and connection with themselves, their communities and ultimately with the earth. This book invites us to see what is possible when we combine successful models: the enrichment and expansion of both the paradigms and the people operating within them. I encourage you to accept the invitation and enjoy the new insights you will undoubtedly come away with.

I have great hopes for this world when our authors and thinkers lead us in the effort of merging effective models. It is with these new ways of thinking about whole selves—the spiritual and the temporal— that I believe we can co-create the healthy and beautiful world we all desire.

Henry Kimsey-House
Co-Author of *Co-Active Coaching* and
Co-Founder of The Coaches Training Institute

PREFACE

*The personal life deeply lived always expands into truths
beyond itself.*

Anais Nin

I want to introduce you to two good friends with this book.
One is Buddhism, the other is coaching. Buddhism has
given me an experience of practical spirituality. I gave
up on the Judeo-Christian conception of God and organized
religion a long time ago, but my soul was not satisfied. In the
Noble Eightfold Path and the other tenets of Buddhism, I
found spiritual guidance that really spoke to my life with its
annoying job, out-of-balance checkbook and its two weeks of
vacation. I did not find it to be electrifying, like say, gospel
music, but it made sense and sense made peace. Coaching,
on the other hand, gave me the experience with grown-
up electricity that Buddhism could not. I feel that like-a-
kid aliveness when I connect with my coach or my clients.
Coaching brought me back to my big, wide-open heart and
brought life back to my life. Separately they are great, but
together they are more.

In this book readers will find an introduction to the basics of Buddhism and see ways to explore it in the context of coaching. If you're a coach, I hope you will see how the *dharma*[1], the core principles of Buddhism, can help you see your clients and your practice from a place of peace and calm. It is not always easy to remain calm when your client changes focus in the middle of the coaching or wants to talk about something small and apparently meaningless when huge questions loom overhead. Buddhism provides a way to look at these experiences that makes sense and creates serenity. It also gives new depth and meaning to the tools coaches already work with. Seeing the synergy between the ancient philosophy of Buddhism and the modern practice of coaching gives us a better understanding of the power of these tools and allows us to be more intelligent about our choice of tools when working with clients. My hope is that we will be better able to see where we are, place ourselves in context, and move gracefully forward, or inward as the moment requires. Working this way, all coaching experiences come to be defined by acceptance and ease, and all outcomes can be held as useful and seen for the growth potential they offer. Working this way, the coaching engagement becomes a *sangha* (Sanskrit for "virtuous community") of two—a place where the focus is on training the mind to seek and promote growth.

If you are not a coach, I imagine you are here because you are a seeker of some sort. You want to develop yourself as a human being, but you don't have the means or the inclination to live in a remote monastery in Asia for any length of time. You're interested in having more in life and that more is not necessarily a material thing. I don't know that you can attain enlightenment on the bus, but you can make a start at it. And coaching can be part of that start. Many people harbor the misconception that coaching is about pursuing materialistic goals. Certainly it can be. But it can be so much more. If you choose to, you can make a sangha for yourself with a coach and create a place to take the events of daily life and start to do exactly what the Buddha prescribed to attain enlightenment—examine them with curious intention to create a shift toward growth and peace. By illuminating this alignment, I hope the book will open the coaching door to more seekers.

For Buddhism in this era, I believe the question of desire will be at the forefront. The exploration is well under way and, for those interested in more in-depth discourse on that subject, I recommend *Open to Desire*, by Mark Epstein, M.D. The context of coaching brings that question front and center and puts as fine a point on it as possible, allowing one person's desire to be the fulcrum for learning and acting in ways consistent with the highest personal growth. And in the end it I think it serves personal growth to pay attention to our desires and in turn our personal growth provides a springboard to more spiritual development.

For coaching, I think the question is about elevating the pursuits of people who are not monks or nuns beyond the ego to a higher plane. We know it is not enough to pursue power, material gain and personal satisfaction for its own sake. Using Buddhist principles, a client's pursuit of money, for example, has the potential to become transformed from a harmful lust to a liberating force. An aware coach can ask, "What is the money for? Whom can it serve? What else can it do?" These are the kinds of questions that can take the acquisition of money, among other things, to a higher plane. The alignment with Buddhism lends resonance and validation to coaching's message that we can and should live fulfilled lives in every moment, with every choice, every single day. An understanding of how ancient philosophies and spiritual guidance can shape the practice of coaching adds depth and meaning to the profession.

Having said what the book is about and what it hopes to be, let me say what it is not. It is not a definitive or teaching text about either Buddhism or coaching. The basic concepts of Buddhism are discussed in simplified ways and a few stories about the Buddha's life are included to give non-Buddhist readers enough to appreciate and follow the discussion. But for a thorough understanding of the concepts of Buddhism and how they apply in modern life, *Awakening the Buddha Within,* by Lama Surya Das, is an excellent resource. The book provides a good overview of all the aspects of the Noble Eightfold Path and the other core tenets of Buddhism and relates them to contemporary life. It also touches on the different schools of thought within Buddhism and gives readers a sense of the subtle but meaningful differences in the various approaches to the same doctrines. I found that the Noble Eightfold Path broadened my spiritual perspective and opened me up to new ways of approaching all aspects of my life. It was here that I first encountered the concept of Right Work and using this philosophical base, I was able to see my way to a major career change, from being a lawyer to being a coach and a writer. In the dharma, I found ways to understand all the questions of everyday life and live the answers with more integrity, more purpose, and less effort.

With respect to coaching, *Co-Active Coaching,* by Laura Whitworth, Henry Kimsey-House, and Phil Sandahl is the best resource for understanding the process. Laura Whitworth and Henry Kimsey-House pioneered co-active coaching, a type of coaching which is defined in large part by its commitment to be neither consulting nor therapy. Co-active coaching is not about a coach giving a client the answer, nor is it about delving into the past and figuring out "why." Co-active coaches believe that clients have the answers because they are naturally creative, resourceful, and whole. From this place, a co-active coach and his or her client design an alliance to engage with the important questions arising from any and all realms of the client's life. There is no one method; there are no checklists and that is one reason why coaching melds with Buddhist philosophy so well. It is all about what shows up *in the moment* and being with it.

I have drawn a great deal from my experiences with clients as well as from my experience as a client. I use these experiences with permission, to illustrate the ways Buddhism has shown me to be more effective with my clients and more relaxed about my practice. The vignettes are not presented in chronological order, and the dialogue is reconstructed from recollection and notes of telephone conversations, the method I use almost exclusively to coach and be coached. I also eliminated identifying facts to maintain my confidentiality agreements with my clients. English, like all languages, has limits, including its arcane rule regarding pronouns and gender. I avoid this where possible by using the plural form, and when I cannot I have opted to alternate between he and she for balance.

Let me clear about this: I do not believe coaching alone is a way to attain enlightenment. And I do not think spiritual growth belongs exclusively in a silent, monastic setting. I think that we can make practical use of the Buddhist philosophy within the context of coaching and when we do, I believe we come closer to enlightenment. The experience of deep fulfillment, the goal of coaching, foreshadows the experience of enlightenment and, I dare say, from time to time, lets us taste it. Coaching is one way to cultivate the beliefs, attitudes and practices that provide a foundation from which a person can pursue and attain the Buddhist concept of enlightenment. Buddhism is more than meditation. It is one of the most vital philosophies ever articulated because it is fully accessible to anyone regardless of their religious or spiritual practice. When the basic principles of Buddhism are applied to coaching, they liberate both coach and client, affording each the opportunity to evolve as individuals and bringing them both to new places in their lives. This is what I want for everyone engaged in coaching: an evolutionary experience that leads to liberation.

1

Commitments—Buddha, Dharma, and Sangha

I go for refuge in the Buddha, the enlightened teacher;
I commit myself to enlightenment.
I go for refuge in the Dharma, the spiritual teachings;
I commit myself to the truth as it is.
I go for refuge in the Sangha, the spiritual community;
I commit myself to living the enlightened life.

The Refuge Prayer

Taking refuge is the first formal step on the journey to enlightenment for most Buddhists. By reciting the refuge prayer, one makes a formal commitment to the Three Jewels of Buddhism: the *Buddha* (the embodiment of wakefulness), the *Dharma* (the teachings of the Buddha), and the *Sangha* (the spiritual community). Though not thought of as "taking refuge" in the traditional Buddhist sense, engaging in co-active coaching is a similar type of commitment. Both the coach and the client assume a Buddha-like relationship with each other. They embody for each other a decision to awaken to the fullness of their lives and they become teachers to one another. They pursue the truth relentlessly in their goal to create life-changing shifts. And they are community for one another in the process.

Both coach and client will have many opportunities to practice the dharma within the coaching engagement. I was once told by the abbot of the Plum Mountain Temple in Seattle who officiated my wedding that everyone is a Buddhist, but some people don't know it yet. The dharma practice that transpires unrecognized within many coaching interactions is living proof of this assertion. The synergy between the two paradigms is such that neither one may realize they are engaged in dharma practice, but the fact that it goes unrecognized does not mean it's not happening. Recognizing the dharma in action, however, adds a depth and meaning to the relationship and its special work. When coaches and clients can see themselves within the context of the Buddhist tradition, more timeless wisdom opens up to each of them. It also expands the mission of coaching beyond the pursuit of worldly goals to the full awakening of the spirit. The Buddhist traditions, once they are seen within coaching, shed a light on the work that extends the full length of the spectrum and produces a calming effect. The relationship then becomes a "sangha of two," a community where the stuff of an ordinary life with all its debris and irritants becomes a lustrous pearl. The coach and client don't need to recognize the synergy between Buddhism and many coaching tools; it's just richer and offers more room for expansion if they do. This chapter explores how the co-active coaching relationship mirrors the act of taking refuge.

***

The Buddha, Prince Siddhartha Gautama, was born 563 b.c.e. in the foothills of the Himalayas. Born into a wealthy royal family, he led an idyllic life until the age of twenty-nine. Then he saw four things that brought him out of his sheltered world and into full connection with humanity: a sick man, a poor man, a beggar, and a corpse. These sights moved him so deeply that he decided to renounce his privileged way of life, his position in society, and a future filled with material comfort in order to resolve the question of suffering that these sights had provoked within him.

In the beginning he devoted himself to a life of extreme asceticism, nearly starving to death in the process. He studied with several teachers, including one who taught through the metaphor of music. This teacher pointed out to him that if the strings on an instrument are set too tight, the instrument will not play harmoniously. But if the strings are set too loose, the instrument will not produce music. Only the middle way, neither too tight nor too loose, produces pleasant music. This insight changed Siddhartha's path. He abandoned the ascetic life and focused on living what he called "the Middle Way"—a path between the values of his former life, which was completely focused on temporal and material well-being, and his ascetic life, which was completely focused on self-denial. He developed the practice of attending to the present moment with singular awareness, and as a result he attained enlightenment, a state called nirvana in which attachment to the ego—with its grasping, aversion, and indifference, and all the suffering that goes with that—had completely ceased. He could have chosen to enjoy this state of mind on his own, but instead, he began traveling around with a small group of followers, speaking to others about what he had discovered. He articulated a set of core principles, including the Four Noble Truths. The Fourth Noble Truth, which describes the way to end suffering, is more fully explained in the Noble Eightfold Path. The Buddha never claimed to be a savior, nor did he expect others to worship him or to adopt his beliefs without applying their own reason. Rather, he taught that it is up to each of us to free ourselves and that this was entirely possible using the tools he had discovered.

After his awakening, the Buddha helped people along the path to enlightenment by coaching them. There is a parable recounted in *Awakening the Buddha Within* about how the Buddha worked with a wealthy man who could not give up or share any of his wealth or possessions. It illustrates a way of engaging with others that is found in coaching. The Buddha told the man to begin by thinking of his hands as belonging to two separate people and to practice generosity by using one hand to give to the other. Gradually the man increased the sums of money moving from one hand to the other. As he saw the man progressing, the Buddha instructed him to soften his heart and to begin making small gifts of money and possessions to family members, then to friends, and finally to beggars and strangers. As he practiced giving, the man became more happy, more free, and more content—in other words, more enlightened.[2]

The Buddha did not ask the man to delve into his past to determine why he had become so miserly. He did not approach the man with judgment about his behavior or dogmatic instruction on how to change. He simply came to the relationship with the intent to shift the man toward enlightenment, creating a sangha of two where the man could study his own behavior and change it through the cultivation of self-awareness. That is coaching.

Although coaches have not attained the Buddha's level of enlightenment, their presence in the engagement brings their intentions in line with those of the Buddha. The word *buddha* means "awakened one." Everyone engaged in coaching, whether as a client or a coach, is awakening to his or her life through the cultivation of self-awareness. To engage a coach or become a coach is in itself a form of renunciation similar to the initial step of the Buddha's journey. By entering into this relationship both the client and the coach must renounce the status quo. The coach is declaring that no one should live a small, dull, "good enough" life; the client is declaring that he or she won't. It is "no" to business as usual and "yes" to a life of expansion, growth, and fulfillment. Like the Buddha and his students, coaches and their clients come to this work with intent to create forward shifts, or at least neutral spaces where self-awareness can create enlightened change. They are acknowledging their mutual renunciation of "passable" lives just passing by and championing a new, full aliveness in every moment of every day. In this way, coaches and their clients, in tandem with the Buddha and his students, are walking the road toward enlightenment.

***

My coach and I are driving from Seattle to Vancouver, B.C. We have decided to attend a function sponsored by the company that delivered our coach training. I am ambivalent about going. I hate these kinds of gatherings, generally speaking. I am not comfortable in large crowds, and small talk quickly bores me. But this crowd will include many people I trained with, and I am looking forward to seeing them. And the talk among coaches, for the most part, isn't small. What ultimately persuades me to go is the fact that one of the creators of the coach training program and a founder of the company is going to be there.

The training made such a profound difference in my life; it is hard to believe it was created by another human being. I want to meet him. I want to see if he is as human as I am. I harbor a subconscious hope that I can be human and still create something significant and that maybe something of his power to do this will rub off on me. That would make any amount of small talk worthwhile.

Though it is almost five o'clock when we arrive in Vancouver, it is a gorgeous, sunny summer evening. The sun is just starting to set, and the top floor of the hotel event room is bathed in a golden glow. I am enjoying the company, and while the event is better than the usual big-crowd affair, there is a certain inescapable feel to the interactions that comes with having a large number of people in one room. It seems to inflame my sense of awkwardness. I decide to search out the founder in order to make this sense of discomfort bearable.

He is impossible to miss. Standing well over six feet, with the girth of a buddha and long wavy hair that gently blends with his unkempt beard, he is attired in a wild mix of clothes. He has an honest smile and, behind his round glasses, warm eyes. I approach him, and as I do, I sense that he shares my distaste for this milieu; he doesn't look like the kind of person who enjoys cocktail parties as a rule. I talk with him for a few moments. We connect over my equally outspoken paint-splash dress, and somehow within this small exchange he finds my spirit and embraces it. The evening program begins, and we find our respective seats, his at the front of the room, mine beside my coach. I purposefully choose a seat that will allow me to mentally wander off into the glorious sunset should this turn out to be boring, the way many large affairs do.

After some introductory remarks, the founder leads us into a coaching demonstration, showing us a skill for helping clients unpack themselves when they feel overwhelmed, a common occurrence in coaching. The feel of the room begins to shift. Focus goes to the front and stays there. Learning is in progress, and this is enticing enough to ignore the sunset. The founder then guides his demo client, a randomly chosen volunteer from the audience, through a morass of emotionally tangled subjects. I can see she is relieved simply to be able to list them all out loud to someone who is not telling her to stop, someone whose only comment over the course of three minutes is, "What else is in there?" Soon they come to a place where she can focus on the one thing that would really make a difference to her if it changed. They work with it a little more. I watch him. It's not magic. He is just asking a few questions here and there, and at the end of ten minutes she is in a different place. The list of burdens is still there, but she no longer feels burdened. She is back in the driver's seat. The circumstances aren't running her; she is running them.

We break off into pairs and do a little coaching ourselves. The room is now buzzing. Everyone is involved and engaged. That "big crowd" awkward feel is gone. There is a new feel now. It is one of aliveness and uplift. We are all in a different place than when we started. On the drive home I think about the founder who didn't look like he enjoyed cocktail parties. He could have come here for the gratification of his own ego; there were certainly enough people in the room like me who were there simply because he was there. But that is not why he came. Despite his feelings about cocktail parties, he came to create that shift toward aliveness and uplift. Like the Buddha, he came to share his gifts with us, to shift our practices into a different place, to help us help our clients.

***

"You should call her," my friend urges. "You'll really like her."

I hold the name and phone number in my hand and think about it in much the same way I have been thinking about many things since I quit my job several months ago. I have been hard at work on a novel, reveling in my unfettered days, but the anxiety of being jobless and without money of my own is interfering. I berate myself for a few minutes. *You're smart enough to figure this out by yourself; you're just being lazy. Do you really think she knows something you don't know?* But today the inner critic is losing. If I really was that smart and I really did know everything I needed to know, I wouldn't be feeling as adrift as I do. I'd have a job by now. I decide to call her. What can it hurt?

Now I am standing on her doorstep, being ushered into her clean, comfortable home. I tell myself she must have cleaned her house for me; no one really lives this way. I search her blue eyes for some sign of what I'm in for. I find competence, assuredness, professionalism, and ease, but no sign of what I am in for. We sit down and talk about confidentiality and coaching in general. She has answered my questions, and still, the only thing I am sure of is that I have no idea what's coming next.

She asks me which area of my life could stand a little bit of rigorous examination. I mull over the invitation. She's already assured me it is confidential. I can say anything. I ask if there are certain topics that are not appropriate for coaching. She says not to worry about it and to just toss out whatever's on my mind. I decide to test her. I have spent the better part of my life controlling my emotions in an effort to protect others. And I know that my emotions are running high as I struggle to find meaningful work. I am not going to pay hundreds of dollars to someone I have to protect. If she can't handle the roiling emotions within me, I need to know now.

I take a breath and hand her the heaviest lead weight I can find in my pockets—my sex life. She doesn't flinch. It's as if everyone does this with her. At some point a few tears roll down my cheeks. She points out the box of tissues on a side table should I want one. I help myself to a few and we carry on. At the end of our conversation I am able to see what I really need to know: she can take it. There is space here for anything I choose to bring up. I remember thinking, on the way home, that we did not make much headway on the topic; indeed she missed a great deal of what I really meant, but I didn't care at all. Like the Buddha, she had made a space for me, a space where I could look at the most volatile aspects of my life in safety and privacy, a place where, like the miserly man the Buddha coached, I could expose and work with aspects of myself that would not necessarily be welcome everywhere.

***

The word *dharma* is most often used to refer to the teachings of the Buddha, but it means much more than this. Literally, it translates as "that which supports or upholds." It also means "that which remedies, heals, and restores." But Lama Surya Das describes it best when he says that the dharma is "the most abundant gift of wisdom . . . it benefits both the giver and the receiver."[3] There is dharma practice for both the coach and client in every situation. Everything from the smallest issue (a client who is always five minutes late) to the biggest issue (a client who is trying to change the world with his work) is grist for the mill, both philosophically and practically. The perpetually late client, for example, may need a lesson in present-moment awareness, while his coach, by means of the same interaction, can explore the concept of idiot compassion or attachment. There is always a lesson for both. It is in this sense that the dharma brings many gifts to the context of coaching interactions.

***

My client does not know what she wants coaching on tonight. I have my opinions about the things we could be pursuing; I think she has room for a much bigger life.

But it's her agenda that counts here, not mine. I usher my opinions into the wings, where they belong, and wait to see what emerges. I toss out an open-ended question to turn on the internal spotlights, to prime the pump. "What's been on your mind?" We begin talking, and it comes forward.

"It's a small thing, really," she says hesitantly, as if it is not worth the time or the attention. "I want to stop swearing. I was listening to myself the other day, and I was sort of shocked. I have a potty mouth!" she exclaims, laughing at the use of the childish word. This may be the thing I love most about coaching; it is where the mundane reveals the sacred. It is where the rubber of philosophy meets the road called life.

"What does that say about you?"

"I think other people think I'm sort of harsh or tacky. Classless. And I'm not. I don't think I look good at all."

"Forget about other people. What do you think it says about you?"

She pauses to consider it from the other point of view. "I think it says the same thing: harsh, tacky, and classless."

"What's true about you?"

There is another pause. It isn't often that we stop to think of ourselves this way, let alone speak of ourselves this way to someone else.

"I think I'm genuine. I think I really have a big heart and I'm outgoing. I think I'm somebody other people can really connect to and like. I'm a good friend."

This is all true, so far as I can observe.

"How do you speak those attributes?"

"Certainly not with swearing." She is starting to see it for the incongruity that it really is, far more than if she simply accepted that it looks bad to other people. It's more compelling if it looks bad to oneself.

"When does it come up the most?"

"When I'm out in social situations. I never do it at work. I think it's me trying to be funny or something. Or prove something?" A tone of wonder has come into her voice, as if she is under the bed with a flashlight realizing there are things there she never suspected, or that they look completely different from how she imagined.

"Why would I do that?" She's asking herself, not me.

"Why" is not really my department. It is the territory of psychiatrists. I look elsewhere. "Let's run a little movie: Imagine yourself out to dinner with a bunch of friends, perhaps some new people. Imagine yourself in conversation; watch yourself work up to swearing. Watch it again in slow motion, frame by frame. What do you see?"

"It is for emphasis or a laugh. That's exactly what I am doing."

"You are emphatic and funny, just in your being," I tell her. "What if you just trusted that?"

It takes a moment to sink in. I say it again.

"Wow, I just totally relaxed," she says.

"Great. Now take that feeling into your movie. Let's play

it again." I guide her through it: "There you are at the table, lots of friends, some new people, and a cute guy you want to impress. You are emphatic and funny, just in your being. Look at your big smile. See your warm eyes?" I continue speaking softly and slowly, periodically punctuating with, "There you are relaxing as you speak. You say something funny, the conversation moves around. There you are." She is quiet.

"No urge to swear. None," she says.

"How can you remind yourself to relax in that moment?"

"Now, that is a good question. I'll have to think about it."

We talk about what is accessible to her from a place of feeling relaxed in her being. She sees that it would be easier to maintain genuine connections to others; that she would be more likely to find the kind of relationship she so dearly wants to be in; and that she could interact better with her work team and get better results from them. It's an enticing picture, and worth finding a way to lock it into place. So I ask her to think of something small that has a sensual component to it—such as a song, a color, or a picture—something that symbolizes the quality of ease with herself. With this anchor at her disposal she can remind herself of this quality and access it at will.

While she is locking her learning into place I lock mine in too, starting with the fact that I needed to suspend judgment as to what we should be talking about. No subject is too small to be meaningful. There is something of the sacred in everything if one looks with a curious eye. And the "big" subjects will always find their way to our focus if that is what we are meant to be looking at. I am reminded of the great power in introspection; awareness precedes every conscious shift. Finally, I acknowledge and thank whatever forces have brought me to this point, where another person is willing to reveal herself to me, to allow me to look inside with her. This is right work for me and I am grateful.

In just thirty minutes we both had meaningful practice with the dharma. This is not to say that coaching is enough to take a person to enlightenment. There are eight prongs on the path mapped out by the Buddha, and Right Work (my work, in this instance) and Right Speech (her work, in this instance) are only two of them. Still, I am amazed and reminded again how well the dharma fits into and guides my life and my work.

***

The word *sangha* is Sanskrit and can be translated as "virtuous community." Though the term originally referred to the communities of ordained monks and nuns, as Buddhism continues to spread throughout the Western world this meaning has changed and expanded. Sangha can be found wherever two or more people convene with the intent to direct their energies toward enlightenment.

This happens in all sorts of places, and when it happens in coaching relationships something truly beautiful blooms for both people.

At the center of the co-active coaching relationship is the client and his or her life balance, life process and fulfillment. Encircling the client is the designed alliance with the coach and the matrix from which the coach is operating: curiosity, listening, intuition, action/learning, and self-management.

When we overlay this model with the concept of sangha, the co-active coaching relationship becomes a source of refuge, a place where the client can take his or her true self, however flawed, unattractive, glorious, vain, or brilliant, and examine it without judgment. It is a place where clients can safely experiment, fail, and experiment again without unmanageable consequences. Incorporating the idea of sangha creates a place for coaches, too, and acknowledges their role in the interaction as well as the intangible benefit they receive from it. And like a Buddhist sangha, the coaching relationship invites both dharma practice and training of the mind. Everything in life, from swearing to soaring, can be an occasion for dharma practice. And as the coach and client develop new ways of approaching the client's life, they train the client's mind to reject limiting beliefs and to integrate new beliefs that spur fulfilling actions. Including the concept of sangha more fully underlines the value of suspending judgment from both sides and creates an environment in which both parties look forward to the unexpected. This in turn liberates both the coach and the client from the pressure of attaining a particular result. Every "flaw" or missed goal can then become a way to grow and learn. Every result, whether desired or not, can then become something valuable.

While each participant can practice living the dharma and growing toward enlightenment, this is a by-product for the coach, not an agenda. Lamas, abbots, and other leaders of spiritual communities do the same; they, too, place the benefits to the community foremost, receiving benefit for themselves only as a secondary effect. Indeed, this is what engages coaches in the work they do. That it is incidental to the coach makes it no less significant. Rare is the time when I cannot benefit from my clients' learning. From the coach's side, when an issue can be regarded more impersonally, it is much easier to see the steps needed to bring growth and to recognize where fulfillment lies. For example, while saying yes to too many of the wrong things may not be my personal issue at the moment, as I watch my clients work this through in their lives I find myself applying the learning wherever it makes sense for me, because inevitably I am saying yes to something that really needs a no. When I hang up the phone and feel a sense of meaning, purpose, and joy in my work, it keeps me coming back to it. The fact that this is an aside in the co-active model does not diminish its value.

Leaving the coach out of the co-active model is sound as a pedagogical device. The coaching relationship is not about the coach; it is about the client, her balance, her fulfillment, and the processing of her life. This is the foundation for the context of self-management, and it is essential for coaches to understand so they can best serve their clients. It is, however, a device, and as such, it does not square with reality. The coach *is* there and does play an important role. The notion of "sangha" allows us to acknowledge that fact.

***

The sun is shining outside. It is a gorgeous day. I think of a man I used to work with who committed suicide one spring a few years ago. Someone told me at that time that the rate of suicides is highest in the spring because the world is bursting with hope, promise, and beauty, and those who are feeling suicidal find themselves all the more confronted with the hopelessness they feel. As I sit here in my backyard, repetitively twisting a blade of grass, my heart goes out to those who believe this makes sense. I can appreciate that the confrontation with hope might at times be just too much to bear.

For I feel quite hopeless now and I feel sad. I am in limbo. I have become a certified coach; there are no more classes, no more scheduled opportunities to connect with the vibrancy that characterized my coach training. It is just me and a handful of clients. I look backward at my lost law career. I don't miss it or regret what I have done. I don't want to be a judge or a politician anymore. But as I look forward, I see nothing. I had imagined myself as a high-powered coach with a big roster of fun clients, leading workshops, speaking, and writing. But my vision is not materializing and my ability to withstand under productivity is dwindling. I am very harsh on myself right now. I have the time, money, and support that my peers desperately wish they had. Surely it signals some failure on my part, I think, that I have not blasted into the professional pantheon. I am blessed, though, with the good sense to know that I need shelter from myself. I pick up the phone and call my old coach.

I tell him up front that I can't imagine how he will be able to reach me or save me from myself; I am too far gone. I tell him I am ready to quit, but I want to talk with someone who doesn't see things the same way I do, just to be sure I really want to quit. I will know by the end of our conversation. We talk for forty minutes. He is patient and uses just enough linear thinking to keep me engaged without allowing it to run the show. At the end of the forty minutes I have no recollection of what he said to me or I to him, but I know I am not quitting. My vision is still resonate and in tact. I am not about to burn anything down with my passionate fire, but I am moving again, I feel hope again. I am in a better place than when I called. This is the beauty of sangha. Community bolsters one's tolerance for the inevitable ruts in the road.

***

My client has figuratively brought someone to the sangha

with her today: her husband. He sits, in her imagination, on the outskirts of the conversation, sullen, brooding, and struggling. We look at him. We talk about him. We talk about her and him. I steer the focus back to her, but he won't leave and she can't take her eyes off him. I want to purify the space of the sangha; it is not right to talk about someone who is not participating in the discussion. But my efforts are in vain. His presence remains.

And then I realize that there is no other room for this in her life. Her husband cannot have this kind of discussion with her; he is too entrenched in himself and defensive. Her family and friends cannot have this kind of discussion with her because they don't want to know about her feelings of despair or her desire to explore them. So she brings all of this in with her—the feelings, the other people in her life, and their agendas. It feels crowded in here. It is not the purest form of introspection, but there is nowhere else for her to go, no one else with whom to talk about her deepest worry—that she has made a colossal mistake by entering into marriage with this man.

For some time we talk on and off about him, about her and the other people in her life, and about other things. At the end of the time it seems she is only an inch or two closer to resolving matters. Viewing this without the Buddhist lens, one might be tempted to criticize the coaching and call it a loss. No action was taken. With the Buddhist reference point, I see more. I see a growing awareness and an ability to embrace reality. She is now looking at the marriage for what it *is*, and seeing herself in it for who she *is* rather than who she *is not* or whom she wishes she could have been. I won't be present when she casts the final vote on the marriage and her role in it, but that doesn't matter. What matters is that she is cultivating the awareness needed to identify what is fulfilling, right action. We have, in this time, created a space where, for once, no one is judging either her or him or the forces that pulled them together.

***

When coaches and clients come together, they become Buddha-like partners to each other. They bring themselves to the work, renewing a commitment to renounce that which is less than full. They come pursuing change for the sake of growth and fulfillment. They create a space of refuge, where judgment is allowed only in order to reflect upon it and neutralize it. They reflect back to one another a nonstop stream of opportunities to see and enlarge their innate Buddha-nature, and they step toward it by practicing the dharma in a myriad of moments. They are community for one another, commitment embodied by two people in an alliance, company along the path we all travel toward enlightenment.

HOLLY MORRIS BENNET

2

True North—The Buddha Within

*What lies behind us and what lies before us
are tiny matters compared to what lies within us.*

Oliver Wendell Holmes, Sr.

B uddhists believe each person is simply an aggregate
of five components that come together and present to
the world in a particular way given the circumstances
of life. Those components are known in Sanskrit as *the five
skandhas* and they are: form (physical characteristics), feelings
(known to us through our five senses and the faculties of
our minds), perceptions (the results from combining feelings
and sensations with judgments and opinions), intentionality
(our will, our motives) and consciousness (recognition
accomplished by your self as you know it).[4]

All of these components are malleable and shifting. If
you were born to poor parents in Honduras you would have
a different form, different perceptions, etc. than you would

if you were born to wealthy parents in Europe. Your cells routinely die, sluff off of your body and regenerate themselves throughout your life. You are not the same person now that you were last year, last month, or last night. The bottom line in Buddhism is simply this: you are not the person you think you are.[5] The self you believe you are simply does not exist, except in fleeting combinations of the components described above that are continually coming together and rearranging themselves according to cause and effect, or *karma*. You are a process from moment to moment without a fixed soul or an eternal self. This concept of "no-self" is known in Buddhism by the Sanskrit term *anatman*. The absence of that which is malleable, shifting and impermanent is defined as emptiness, or *sunyata*.[6] This emptiness is defined by purity and radiance; it is from this that Buddha-nature arises and to this that Buddha-nature resolves.[7]

If the self as we know it does not exist and what remains when the skandhas fall away is a radiant emptiness, what is the point of coaching? If the point of the practice is to experience non-self fully—to detach from our components and release our grasp on the transient—what is the point of studying the self? One answer is that to experience non-self and nirvana, one must have a firm handle on the self that you are right now. This is why the Noble Eighfold Path is delineated for us, to give us full command of our minds and our actions. You cannot release your grip on something you do not hold or possess in the first place. [8]

This is a very simplified discussion of a complicated set of philosophical issues within Buddhism and each school of thought has a slightly different interpretation of these concepts and how they apply to life. There is, however, within the study of the self to which coaches are committed, an interesting parallel. There is a place within each client which is void of all limitations, a powerful place defined by grace and radiance. From this place, every person can access his or her beautiful, perfected nature and use that inner luminosity to light the way along the path. It is as if all that is best about us is a brilliant pearl obscured by muck and covered over by a hard shell. Through the practice of dharma and by means of coaching tools, we can each open up that shell and wipe away the muck, allowing our best selves to shine. This is our home base, the place we can always return to for redirection and focus.

Here is one of the first points where coaches and clients can realize the synergy that exists between the two disciplines. After all, coaches have a natural impulse to seek out a client's inner radiance. This is the core of what coaching is about, helping people find the part of them that is already perfect and making it shine. One manifestation of this inner radiance is what many co-active coaches call *the future self.* If there is a "true North" for coaching clients, it must be this future self, the person inside who knows the answers, intuitively and without doubt, the person inside who is fully alive without compromise or regret. Access to the future self is a gift of the coaching engagement, and it's one that truly keeps on giving long after the coaching relationship is over. In this chapter we'll see how coaching can help reveal that inner light and see what it looks like when it is shining.

***

I am walking around a park in Seattle, talking to a client about coaching. Lake Washington laps at the edge of the path we walk. Giant shade trees border the other edge, creating just enough shelter from the summer sun. Everyone is out enjoying the weather, babies in strollers, middle-aged women walking in pairs, older people dwarfed by their stereophonic headphones. Daring dog owners have let their canine friends off leash to splash in the lake, risking \$170 fines for the pleasure of seeing their dogs happy the way nature intended.

My client and I sit down on a bench after taking a quick trip around "The Wheel of Life," a ten-section pie chart that has shown us how she grossly measures her satisfaction with the key elements of her life, relationships, environment, job, career, fun, health, and so on. She rates them according to how she feels about each, assigning a low number to money and a high one to health. Her job is in the middle and relationships receive the lowest rating.

"If this was a wheel on your car, what would the ride be like?"

"Pretty uncomfortable," she acknowledges, "it's pretty flat on that one side," she says laughing and pointing to the section about relationships. "But I don't really know what I want to do about any of them."

"Actually, I think you do. In fact, I know you do. You may not know it consciously, but there is a part of you who knows exactly what she wants. My job is simply to reveal that person and her knowledge." It is possible to go through an entire lifetime not realizing we are whole and complete, that we each hold within ourselves an essence that was there before our bodies came into existence. So I make it my personal business to communicate this to as many people as possible.

She considers this. "I don't know. I think there's a lot of stuff that needs fixing."

"Your life may not look or feel the way you want it to at this moment, but there is nothing wrong with you, and nothing in need of fixing. You can make this wheel into anything you want, a flat tire or a Pirelli on a Porsche. You really can." At the time, I don't realize how deeply it is hitting her, but later she tells me how novel it was to think she already had all the answers within herself, that there was actually nothing to fix. From then on she began to see her life work differently, to view it as a project that she could continually observe and adjust. She told me that this one concept alone revolutionized her thoughts and her actions. But she didn't have to say it. We worked together on and off over the course time, and I watched her move from struggling with money to studying to become a financial planner. I watched her stop dating dead-end guys and proceed to get married. I watched her put an end to her unsatisfying living situation and move into her own home. The inner light is amazing; to discover it and live a life guided by it is indeed revolutionary.

***

My friend and I are looking at some of his new art work. We worked together as coach and client a few years ago.

"Hey, Holly, you know that future self thing we did a long time ago? I loved that. Have you got any variations on it I can use now?" He is referring to a visualization exercise we did at the beginning of our coaching three years ago. At the time, employing a widely used, scripted visualization I guided him twenty years ahead into his own future.[9] (This exercise is reprinted in Appendix A.) After guiding him into a very still meditative state, I invited him to go to the home of his future self and take a look around. I asked him to sense the place and the person who inhabited it. He described the home as peaceful and the person in it as wise and balanced. He saw himself and his life not as he wished them to be but how he sensed they could be. He talked to himself in the future and gleaned some sense of his own internal wisdom. When we debriefed the exercise, he described his home and what made it uniquely his. He told me about the evidence he saw of his own accomplishments; it was clear he visualized his triumph over the struggles then plaguing his life. When we finished, we found a chair in his home where he could sit and instantly access this inner person as well as the feelings of peace, control, and certainty he carried within himself.

Now, three years later, I tell him, "Sure, you could take yourself into that same, quiet, meditative state we started with, using a few minutes of relaxation and meditative breathing, then go to the home of your future self for a dinner party. Check out the guests. What kind of people has your future self invited to meet you? What are they doing in life? What kind of conversation are you having? Then when you come back to present time, start looking for those people— what they're up to in the world, what they're talking about. Get close to them and see what happens."

He likes the idea and I tell him I'm glad that the future self tool is still working for him. "Tell me how you use the future self in your meditation now," I ask. He describes a morning ritual that includes ten to thirty minutes of chanting the Buddhist mantra OM MANI PADME HUNG (which translates as "Jewel of Enlightenment is in the Heart Lotus"), something a friend taught him. He has replaced the chair we located in his house with a zafu (a meditation cushion), and from there, after chanting, he takes himself to visit his future self fifteen years into the future. It reminds him, he tells me, that the essence embodied in his future self is not the same as the person who is living his day-to-day life. It is like distinguishing between one's character and one's reputation, he explains. The future self is like his character, the deeper, more constant part; his daily life persona is like his reputation, the layering on top of his future self.

Visiting with his future self reconnects him to the deeper constant within him—his innate Buddha-nature, as I would say—and helps him focus his intention on "what the hell he is doing" as he would say. The results have been amazing. Somewhat reluctant to put this much stock in the power of his own forward focus and intention, he tells me the last ten months have been the most prosperous time in his life, ever. He describes the projects he has completed and the one he just landed. They are the types of things his future self would be doing, befitting of his tremendous gifts as an artist and financially rewarding as well. I know his daily future self visualizations and chanting are integral to the success he is experiencing. He is closer to the vision of his life that we found three years ago, and every step takes him closer.

***

The first thing I see when I wake up in the morning is the elaborate molding on the ceiling. The overhead light rests in a nest of plaster palm leaves. Around that is an ornate ring of Victorian curlicues. The whole thing reminds me of a mandala, the circular design symbolizing the universe that Buddhists and Hindus use as an aid in meditation. In this way, aided by the reminder on my ceiling, I consider my universe anew each morning, setting my internal compass to "true North." It helps me to prioritize against the inevitable circumstantial encroachments of daily life.

This morning I am set on spending quality time with my manuscript. We have been separated for several days now and it needs attention. I have been thinking that it needs more structure—headings and subheads, maybe. My first thought is to take to my desk, but my tiny office is lacking in light, and my future self doesn't do this sort of thing. She seeks out nature. She finds inspiration and access to another dimension of herself in the outdoors. The weather is going to be good today, so I decide to take inspiration from my future self and go outside to sit with and reconnect to my manuscript.

I drop my young daughter off at day care and consider my outdoor options. There is a pretty place close by, which would be convenient, so I drive there to test it out, but it's too cold there right now. I mentally weigh other close-by options and eliminate them all—no benches, too much shade, and so on. I take a moment to connect with my future self and remember that her essence is one of freedom. "Free," the name I call her, refuses to be dominated by time in the same way I am. She points me toward the furthest possible place, a garden I love out on the peninsula. That would be the Free move. My logical mind instantly begins to conjure up all sorts of reasons why I cannot go that far out today.

Then I find myself driving, on autopilot, out to the peninsula gardens. It is the only way I will get there. If I let my rational mind in on this, I will be back in my tiny, dark office trying to squeeze in a load of laundry between the occasional profound thoughts.

I drive into the parking lot of the gardens and my heart soars. The sun is shining brightly out here today. The trees and flowers look spectacular. The air is lightly perfumed and I detect a slight breeze. I find a spot that is neither too sunny nor too shady and tune into the gentle movement of the air. It takes me back to a powerful dream I had about an arch of trees. In the dream I am walking along a path flanked by mature trees. They have grown into an arch over the road, their long branches reaching out toward each other from either side. Their leaves gently rustle in the breeze and I feel as if I am hearing the voice of the divine. I later see the path and the trees as a symbol for the spiritual nature of life's path and every time I am in the presence of arching trees, something moves deep inside me. I listen for that voice of the divine now as I study the pages I have written so far. I come to realize that the book needs exactly the opposite of what I had imagined. It needs less structure, not more. I comply, deleting headings and chapter titles. It loosens up, and the creative flow begins again. The book and I are back in sync. New structure emerges. Things move around. I breathe a sigh of relief. I was afraid that my absence would invite writer's block. And now I remember I always have the ultimate cure inside me—my future self, my Free.

***

Every coach and every client needs a place to come back to when the coaching is lost, off-track, confused. Luckily, as with all the things we ever truly need, that wise, centered place is within us. It is simply a matter of accessing it and using it. When coaches operate from a place of self-management, allowing clients full permission to roam across the landscape of themselves and their environment, then persistently steer them toward North, we each come closer to the person within who embodies our Buddha-nature and expresses the part of us that is innately powerful, wise, and centered. When this happens and we see congruence between the world of the future self and the world we are creating, the book gets written and the big, juicy artistic jobs start happening. If, as a coach, you do nothing other than listen without judgment, constantly striving to connect your client with his or her higher self, you are not only succeeding, you are bringing that person closer to enlightenment—and you are moving there yourself. Only when we know our selves at our core are we prepared to release ourselves into the bliss of nirvana.

3
When is a Corner Really a Door?

*If we could see the miracle of a single flower clearly,
our whole life would change.*

The Buddha

The philosophy of Buddhism is one of the simplest ever articulated. It requires really nothing more than awareness of the present moment. That concentrated effort of awareness is what we call meditation, and it can be undertaken anywhere, anytime. In fact, cultivating this skill in the midst of a busy life is just as valuable as the sitting practice of meditation. Finding your breath and focusing on it without fidgeting while sitting on a cushion in a quiet room is a difficult and valuable skill because it allows you to find that same sense of peace and centered calm when the external world is not cooperating. Wouldn't it be nice to be peaceful while dinner is burning and your spouse is wondering for the hundredth time where the car keys are rather than caught up in the emotional swirl of tension and frustration? This is part of what makes coaching such an attractive platform for cultivating present-moment awareness; clients can be right in the middle of their busy lives and be learning to cultivate present-moment awareness. Whether it's by asking the client to stay attuned to the moment or helping the client to see that moment from a different perspective, coaching can use the tool of present-moment awareness to create life-changing shifts. It proves the adage that we do not need to see new things; we only need to see things in a new way.

***

My client, one of the most naturally creative people I have ever known, is talking about a new project idea. Ideas spring out of her like fireworks at Fourth of July. And, like all her ideas, this is a good one. It makes use of her obvious artistic talent and answers the call of her inner entrepreneur, all at the same time.

"I like this one a lot," she says, "but I don't know if it's the right one." She proceeds to reintroduce a few of her other good ideas, compare them to this one, and commit to none of them.

"Your energy is sagging," I notice.

"It is."

"Your energy is sagging when we're talking about your really good idea. What's up with that?"

"I don't know," she says reflexively. This is her favorite hiding spot.

"You know I don't believe that."

She laughs ruefully. "I know, I know. You think I know."

"I'm certain that you know. What are you noticing as we talk about your ideas?"

"I feel sluggish."

"What's the texture?" I ask, probing this moment of stuckness for more.

"I'm not moving," she says, "it feels like mud."

"Mud."

"Yeah. I'm stuck in this mud." She adds some sound effects to accentuate the gloppy, heavy quality of the moment. I get it.

"Just thinking about which of all your good ideas to choose creates this mud," I notice. I am only stating what's obvious to me, my observation of the present moment.

"It does!" I can hear her sitting bolt upright. "It's not the ideas, it's all this thinking about them and analyzing and worrying."

The feeling of being stuck in the mud is in the background now, and a new moment is before us. I ask, "So what are you noticing now?"

"It's like a light just went on."

"What do you see now?"

"That I could just pick one and quit thinking about it."

"What does that feel like in your body as you say it?"

"Light!" she says, surprised. "Buoyant." There is a moment of silence while this realization sinks in, "Oh, my God. All I have to do is stop thinking." We laugh. Her sparkly mind is so attractive with its creative wonders and all the futures it invites, it is as if she's never realized that she could just turn it off. And we would have missed this if we had tried to step over the mud instead of standing in it for a moment.

***

My husband and I have a friend who climbs rocks for fun. This is a paradox to me: rocks and fun? I don't get that. He has persuaded us to come out to the University of Washington campus rock-climbing wall to have a go at it. So here I am, donning these strange little shoes and hand grips, listening to our friend explain how it's done. I stand before the wall and scope out a route for my first foray. I put my foot in and easily find the first few moves. About a third of the way up, I pause to look for the end point.

"I can't see the end!" I call down. Our friend, who is a kind of coach for me in this moment, doesn't realize that knowing where I'm going is imperative to a hopelessly linear ex-lawyer, and calls back, "Oh, that's okay, Holly, just keep going."

But the end seems far away and, from this odd angle of my body, virtually impossible. I start trying to use my analytical mind to figure out how I will get there. After a few moments I realize I have not moved, and continuing to look at the ever-elusive top is not helping. I return my focus to the awkward place where I am lodged.

I test out some handholds. I don't like any of them.

"These handholds suck!" I call down.

He laughs. "Yeah, that happens sometimes. Just pick one and try it." *Why is he laughing? This isn't funny. They really do all suck.*

I test them again and find one I can live with. This shifts the perspective on the top dramatically. Now the end is completely out of sight. I panic. How will I get there if I can't see it? I don't bother calling down. I know what my coach will say. There is nothing to be done now except look for another handhold. I find one that will allow me to see the goal, but it is a lousy hold. I look for another one. This one is better, but the view does not bring the goal in sight again. I don't like it, but I take it.

"How am I supposed to do this if I can't see where I'm going?" I demand.

He calls back, "You know where you're going. Don't worry about it. I'm telling you, Holly, the top is exactly where you left it." I hear my husband laugh. I'd kick him in the shorts, but then I'd lose my perfect foothold. I focus upward, then in front of me. I instinctively know there is nothing to be gained in looking down, except fear and a headache.

Finally I stop looking for the goal. It comes and goes from view, but that no longer matters to me. I have finally gotten into the groove of looking for and moving into the next move and staying present to that task. At some point I completely forget about the top, and ironically the next move I find brings me right in front of it. I am stunned. Here I've arrived where I wanted to be, yet without really knowing how I managed it. Nevertheless I am exhausted, and I realize I have attacked the task as if there were someone with a stop watch on my butt. My hands hurt and I am breathless. The rock is unmoved.

"I'm so freaking tired," I call down from the top. "You didn't tell me I could hurt myself on this dinky little wall." It really does seem dinky now that I'm on top. It just isn't that far off the ground.

Our friend laughs. "It's not a race, Holly." I laugh too, because my body has sharpened the lesson of present-moment focus. I realize from my physical tiredness that only part of me was really in the moment. Another part of me had her eye firmly fixed on that last moment and she was the one carrying the stop watch. As if to say, *Okay, fine, do this present-moment stuff, but HURRY UP!* She is the one who is exhausted. Not that I wouldn't have been tired in the end, but it would have been a different kind of tired. I make a mental note to myself.

***

I turn to my coach, hating myself for wasting my valuable time with him on this annoying nettle of a problem, but the truth is I am at the bottom of an emotional paper bag and I wouldn't be able to find my way out if someone handed me a blowtorch, a map, and an open door all at once. I have a conference call with my leadership group in a few days, and I am so frustrated with the person leading the call I can hardly contain myself. She and I have struggled, arguing politely by e-mail, but at the end of the day she is leading the call and I am not. I want to be present and participate, yet every time I think about it I see myself spewing venom into the phone lines. This is not who I want to be when I grow up. Every time I try to move beyond our struggle I find myself caught short. I want out of this nasty string of moments!

Though I don't think he would call himself a Buddhist, my coach encourages me to practice the dharma. "Holly, don't build from the past. That moment is gone. You can build from the past if you choose, but what will you create?"

"More of the same," I say glumly. There is no way out of this. *I feel what I feel,* I think stubbornly. My resentment clings to me like twisted plastic wrap.

"What if you come to the call and just participate moment by moment? Just be in the moment and build from whatever alignment you can find in that particular moment?"

I consider this.

"What if I can't find any alignment?" I ask, clinging harder to my resentments.

"You'll simply acknowledge that and look at what comes up in the next moment," he says patiently.

I visualize myself picking up the phone, heart racing, dialing in, waiting, listening, and then relaxing into this task. I face this moment, it goes, another emerges; I face that one, it goes, and so on. I like this idea. It feels manageable. I will just choose what to do in the very moment.

"I can get behind that."

"Good."

"I don't have to think about this one more moment. I just show up and create from the cards I get. What if I get dealt the joker?" I ask.

"Exactly," he says, laughing. There is no need to entertain this question; it will be handled in the moment.

The call has started. I can feel the fury and frustration arise in me as I listen to the woman lead the call. I breathe. Okay, that moment's gone. The frustration evaporates as I listen to the other members of the group. It rises again as I watch my part in creating this call, the part that was useful, go unacknowledged. I almost sink into that moment and lose myself, but like all feelings, it goes away. I am more enthralled actually with being in these very tense, packed moments as an observer. It is what I imagine it would be like to be a very skilled surfer, which I am not; hell, I don't surf at all. But today I do.

My moment to speak comes, and I search myself for feelings. The frustration, anger, and sense of being snubbed are gone. I speak what is there and it is useful to the group. My moment passes, and like a wave washing ashore, I gently blend with the space around me. I stop my intense focus on the moment for a few minutes just to revel in what happened and what did not. There was no venom in the space of our call. Rather, I called forth something far more interesting and creative. And all of it came from simply focusing on the moment at hand and nothing more.

***

The moments described above were not the hardest a client or coach has ever faced, but none of them was particularly fun. My client was not happy to be backed up against the wall by her "I don't know," only to find herself hip deep in mud. I was not happy to be struggling through the moments of anger and frustration described above. And yet they were some of the more illuminating, instructive moments for everyone involved. It is difficult to keep one's focus on such moments, so it is here where a coach can offer some of the most powerful service by modeling the courage necessary to stay with them and by supporting the client to do the same. My coach could have said, "Oh, you'll get over it in time. The feelings will die down," but instead he stood with me where others were not able or willing. Hold these moments like a cup of hot coffee. Carry them like you would that cup of hot coffee if you were walking across the deck of a ship listing in high waves. Sip them and enjoy them.

Very few people do this with the moments of their lives. An ability and willingness can be worth everything to the coaching client, both in that moment and in the future as well.

One of the most powerful tools a coach has is that of facilitating a change in a client's perspective, an undertaking also valued in Buddhism. Buddhists believe that reality is all relative. The circumstances in which we find ourselves are transitory and impermanent. We don't have to leave home to find the experience of the mystical, nor do we have to partake of extreme adventures in order to radically change our perceptions. We can do all of this and more by simply looking with "new" eyes. It is such a simple tool that its power can easily be underestimated. But to guide clients in this way can be amazing. Major, life-changing shifts can be had simply from looking at the moment in front of you in a different way.

***

My client is anxious. Two areas of her life—her business and her relationship—are in flux. I see her as a buoy on choppy waters, tossing from side to side with the motion of the water. I know it is uncomfortable, but I know she will float; she will make it. She doesn't share this perspective. Her confidence is flagging and she sees herself holding on for dear life, about to go down unless something unforeseen happens.

On my end of the phone, I make a pie chart, assigning different perspectives to each section and take notes while we talk. We create metaphors for each of the different areas. We visualize new ways of seeing the same thing—some positive, some more negative, some spiritual, some just plain crazy. In one of them she sees herself succeeding. We call it the "Can Do It" perspective. Here she finds optimism, hope, competence, all the things she needs to move through the transitions before her. She leaves the call with a surge of energy and positivism.

When we talk about this experience later, she tells me the effect: "It was like getting new glasses. The whole world seemed to be a different color when I stayed in that perspective. I started noticing support for it everywhere. I noticed a man jogging up my very steep hill and I heard him muttering, 'I did it,' every few steps. I don't think I would have heard him if I wasn't looking at the world in this different way. I started to see how many things I do with ease in life and I just realized, 'I can do this.' It just started me on a whole different way of looking at things. And nothing changed except me and the way I was seeing it." Seven months later she doubled her income, and now her business is growing. At the same time, her relationship changed direction toward a commitment with future plans.

***

I am talking on the telephone with my coach about how to be successful in this business. The former lawyer who lives within me is still insisting that there is a door somewhere marked, "Hot Coaching Practice" and that if I could just get smart about finding it and doing it, it would be mine consistently rather than sporadically. She invites me to take leave of the lawyer within for a few minutes and tap into her whimsical energy.

"Where are you, darlin'?" she asks.

"At my piano." I am holding my telephone in my left hand and running my right hand over the keyboard. I love this piano, even though I hardly ever play it anymore. My husband plays and our daughter bangs on it, and this makes me happy rather than regretful.

"Okay, what's the "piano" perspective on how to be successful?"

Without thinking I answer, "Well, there are eighty-eight keys on a piano—so there must be a million ways to be successful." I strike a D major chord and progress it up and down a few times. It triggers an extension of the metaphor. "It's like maybe I could combine some things and then it would come together in one way, or I could combine different things and it would come together in a different way." I am brightening up. The world feels freer; there are more possibilities, not less.

We play around with other perspectives and I come up with one called "Big Dog." This is the one where I put all my feisty, fun, happy energy. I combine the eighty-eight keys with Big Dog and I am off, at least for a few days. Like all clients, I run hot and cold at times. The perspective itself, however, lasts three full years in my memory and I pull it out later when I am ready to run hot again. Just a string of moments, but they may underscore an entire lifetime.

***

My client and I are meeting in person. She's from out of town but she's working out at my gym as a guest today. We meet up after working out and find an out-of-the-way couch on the second floor and share it like school chums catching up.

"What's on the agenda for today?" I ask.

"Well," she says, "I've been thinking a lot about my job." She proceeds to articulate her perspective on the job, which I have heard before.

"We've got to shift this," I tell her, "It's such a drain. Look at you. You came in here all bubbles, and now, after two minutes of talking about this job, you're flat as an open can of three-day-old Coke. Are you game to find some other ways of looking at this?"

"Definitely," she agrees. It's old to her too.

We pop off the couch and start creating metaphorical perspectives on the job based on whatever is at hand: a painting of a boat—she thinks of coasting, just gliding along and focusing on other things; a plant—she thinks of the ways in which this job no longer grows her as a person; the couch—she thinks of how easy it is in some ways to just go in, put in her time, and then walk out the door with a nice little retirement. We physically stand in each perspective and explore it emotionally, trying to see what it would be like if this was the perspective she had in connection to her job. Three quarters of the way through, we land in a corner.

"What's the "corner" perspective on the job?" I ask.

There is a sharp intake of breath and a pause. "I just saw myself crouching in the corner like a caged animal, snarling and straining to get free, trapped and dying."

We stay with this for several more moments, exploring the contours of the ugliness, letting the despair sink in. She is near tears, which tells me she now understands, at that unforgettable body level, how this perspective looks and feels. We move on to other perspectives, but this one haunts her.

There is an urge, especially at the beginning of one's career, to want to leave clients feeling better than when they came. The logical mind thinks they won't come back; we feel badly for their pain; our wallets cling to their wallets because our livelihoods are inextricably linked to their checkbooks. The baseline principles of self-management and client wholeness provide a firm place to stand in those moments, but Buddhism and the belief that each client is equipped with an indestructible inner light can give us something more: faith. Both paradigms see the client as having the inner resources to make the journey, wherever that journey is going. If you are running a marathon, the shoes you need will be provided. And if you don't have shoes, it's because not having shoes is part of your journey.

We don't meet again before she leaves Seattle, so our next connection happens by telephone a week later. Even with this knowledge, it is a long week. I want to call her and see how the process is unfolding, but I stifle this urge. It isn't my process. There is nothing I can add right now, and my disturbance of her process, however well intentioned, may take something away from it. I wait. When she calls the next week, the process has run its course. She has decided: "I feel like I've seen the future in a crystal ball. I know what I will become if I stay in that corner and I can't do that to myself. I have to leave. All we have to do is figure out when."

As coaches, we are in a unique position to help our clients see the miracles before them in every moment, especially those apparently useless moments of frustration. By staying tuned to the moment and using fresh perspectives to reexamine those moments, we can, as the Buddha said, witness the miraculous.

4

Still the Mind, Open the Gate

True silence is the rest of the mind, and is to the spirit what sleep is to the body, nourishment and refreshment.

William Penn

Every coach and every Buddhist knows that progress toward fulfillment or enlightenment depends on training the mind, coming to grips with its unruliness, managing and regulating its content and focal points, and periodically interrupting and shutting off its machinations. Meditation is the tool commonly used in Buddhist practice, and though traditional meditation is not typically used in the context of coaching, it does provide a valuable resource for learning how to manage our busy minds. This chapter explores three ways of calming the mind within the context of coaching and the rewards that come with that silence.

***

My client is a chatterbox, both internally and externally. When we first meet, I find it difficult to get a word in edgewise and I wonder whether she is someone I should work with at all. She is incredibly fun and funny, so I open myself to learning whatever she has to teach me and I schedule another call. As I work with her, I am stunned by her capacity to fill the space with words. Then I realize she is just one of those people who is 100 percent transparent; she simply speaks whatever is on her mind. All the time.

The problem with her chatter is that most of it is highly negative, self-deprecating, and emotionally fatiguing to her. It is so pervasive that she is completely unaware of it, but in less than two hours I see how ferociously this dynamic shuts her down and cuts her off from realizing her full potential. This negative deluge has to stop, but neither of us can turn the engine off. The very act of speaking, which is the vehicle for most telephone coaching, starts the engine up and then there is no stopping it.

Just when I am about to give up, I find a tool we can use to engage her mouth in service of calming her mind—the mantra. The word *mantra* is Sanskrit for "something to lean the mind upon."[10] Mantras allow the mind to rest by having the chanter say the same thing over and over again, without any need to think at all.

"You can't say yes to everything, you know, yet you say yes all the time," I observe.

"I know. But what else can I say?"

"Great question. What's the answer?"

"Well, there isn't anything else to say! I need the money, I can't say no. I don't want to disappoint her, she just can't take it. She's not used to it."

"I can think of at least three things you could say. You wanna hear them?" I offer.

"Yes! What else can I say?"

"'No.' You could just say 'no.'"

She laughs.

"Okay. Too Nancy Reagan. I know how you feel about her. You could say 'maybe.'"

She giggles again.

"You could say, 'Ask me on Wednesday and I'll let you know.'"

She laughs again. "Okay, okay. I get your point."

"Here's one you might find more comfortable: 'I'd love to say yes, but I have to say no.'"

"I'd love to say yes, but I have to say no," she practices. We both notice how it flows off the tongue. She can do this.

"Say it again."

She practices this four or five times, until it just rolls off her tongue with no effort, and more important, no thought. Her mind can rest while her mouth automatically rolls out these few little words.

"It's easy!" she declares. Victory is hers.

"What will you do when she presses you? You have to assume that she will press you," I say, knowing full well how domineering her boss is.

"I'll just say it again and again." She laughs. "She'll be thinking I've gone crazy, but eventually she'll quit asking." My client has a great sense of humor, and I love the way she has invoked one of her best strategies in her own favor. She can use this to mentally reinforce the magic of the mantra. We speak again the following week. Her mind is so enjoying its vacation from over thinking that she has conjured up another mantra to keep petty tasks from encroaching on her precious time—one that I've borrowed from her and use all the time now—"The best part of my day belongs to me."

***

Meditation is the most common form of mind training used by Buddhists. Usually it is undertaken while sitting in silence. The goal is to stem the stream of thoughts and create mental clarity by focusing on one's breathing. Certainly a coach and client can meditate together, if that is their agenda. But most clients are not going to pay coaching fees to sit on the phone in silence. Still, the mental spaciousness and clarity of a meditative state can easily be created and incorporated into a typical coaching call in just a few moments.

***

I have come to this call from a chaotic schedule mess—canceled calls, double-booked calls that turned out to be triple-booked—and I am squeezing this into a tiny window of time when my daughter is out at the park with her babysitter. My coach tells me to take a moment and get present to our call, and I say yes, but I don't actually do it. My mind is racing and it can't stop. I jump right in, talking about a project I am working on. "It's flat," I tell him, "and I can't decide if the problem is me, the project, or the circumstances."

He laughs softly, and then, speaking slowly like a hypnotist, he mentally transports me to the beach for a walk with my future self. He invites me to feel the sand beneath my feet and to hear the roar of the surf in my ears as I walk side by side with my future self, experiencing the wind in our hair, with nowhere to go, nothing to do. My feverish thoughts stop racing, my heart slows down, and my breath becomes calm. He is engaging me in a meditative state without instructing me to meditate. It works. There is now more clarity and space. From this calm and centered position I am able to access my inner truth about the project and from there expand to the larger truth I learned on the rock wall years ago: forget the end point, just find the next handhold. Could I have done this myself? Of course I could have, eventually. But until I connected with my coach in the moment I came to the call, I was so entangled in my own chaotic, overshooting, off-target, hyperactive energy that I wasn't even able to remember what to do. To me this recalls the power of sangha. With my coach alongside me, I don't have to think of everything myself. He is able to hand me bits of dharma wisdom and I practice as we move along together.

***

The power of silence should not be overlooked. What is available to us in silence? At least two things: (a) awareness of the workings of the mind and how the mind can work against us; and, (b) a greater awareness of the body's wisdom and its messages. This is something that coaches and clients can try to use for themselves and with each other because there is always some space in between calls or meetings where the power of silence can be found.

***

Our leadership group has come to the end of a long day, finished dinner, and convened in the main room. After we settle in, our retreat leaders announce that we'll be spending the next twenty-four hours in silence, beginning tonight. A silent shock jolts the room, and I am simultaneously horrified and fascinated. I only meditate occasionally, and my belief that I should achieve some extraordinary state of mind or profound insight upon rising from my cushion is usually disappointed. The main thing I've achieved is the awareness that I have an extraordinarily unruly mind. Still, I have always wanted to explore maintaining a longer period of silence, so now the moment is at hand.

We retire to our beds without speaking to one another. I sleep in an agitated state and wake up several hours earlier than usual. Out on the deck of the retreat center with a glass of milk and some toast, I revel in the early morning. I remember that as much as I enjoy a good sleep, I do love the quiet of the early morning, the peace of my solitude, the chance to see the sun coming up and hear the last of the night sounds. It is especially pleasant here, in the semi-rural setting of northern California. The moon sinks behind a towering sequoia as bands of pink and orange streak the sky. The wooden deck is slick with dew. And for once, no human voice interrupts the voice of nature. Eventually other people rise, quietly get their breakfast, and join me outside. The sounds of nature's awakening are now robust and full. I marvel at how much I have missed in the rush of the other mornings.

We go into the main room to meditate for twenty minutes. It sounds so simple, but once seated on the cushion, a physical resistance rises in me that is almost agonizing. I can still my mind, I can breathe and focus only on my breath, but the challenge of doing this for an extended period of time while seated seems Herculean. I notice how much I want to fidget, but I don't want to let my group down by being a distraction. I notice all my other litany of anxieties, and as I do, I am rather surprised. I sound neurotic in here. It's as if I have entered a strange echo chamber where my hearing range has expanded and I am now detecting all sorts of sounds that I usually miss. I make a mental note of this, the first of many.

We engage in various activities throughout the day, both alone and as a group, and as the time passes, I find I have no urge to speak at all. The silence is so much more engaging. I continue to watch my mind and notice how petty and repetitive my thoughts can be. I admire their prolific nature, however; it is a ceaseless stream, though most of it is garbage. Periodically an insight emerges like a beautiful sea creature coming to the surface for a breath of air. I train my focus on it and try to grasp it before it recedes into the ocean of my mind again.

Finally, I see how stunning and brutally distracting my thoughts are. I review what I have thought about all day and see only a few things truly worth keeping and building a life around. As I look at my thoughts, I realize why my books can't get written, why my coaching practice soars and plummets like a roller coaster, why my other creative urges go unmanifested: I am too distracted by the dust swirling around in my own mind. I feel like I have been watching dust devils—tiny, harmless cyclones—all day long and am now covered in debris and blinded by the irritating particles. No wonder I am often at loose ends. I live in a wind-whipped dust bowl. At the end of the day, I crave the continuation of silence. I don't want to hear myself speak, or anyone else for that matter. I don't write in my journal. I realize how much value I have always put in words, how attached I am to their power, yet how often they have failed me.

As a group we each emerge from our silence mindfully. I speak only a few words at a time, and then very quietly as others around me do the same. The silence breaks around us like thin ice on a pond, cracking into a jagged mosaic.

***

After my day of silence and my opportunity to see how the mind can work against even the most determined person, I have a call with one of my clients. She has a brilliant mind and it's killing her. Simultaneously her best friend and her worst enemy, it generates beautiful ideas, then cuts them down faster than the Iron Chef with forty ginsu knives. It doesn't even have to wait for the good idea; if she even comes up with a good *feeling* about an idea, the mind is there to kill it. It is astonishing to watch. This dilemma has to end. The machete-like action of her mind makes mine look tame.

She tells me, "I even have a name for the blog or website or whatever. But I'd have to get a designer, and that costs money."

"Tell me the name of your idea before you kill it."

"What?"

"The idea. It hasn't even lasted five full seconds. You've said nothing more about it than that it exists as an idea, and now you're killing it."

She laughs, but it's not because she finds it funny. She tells me the name. It is catchy and it fits her. Then she adds, "I know, it's kind of cheesy-sounding isn't it?"

"You're killing it again."

"I know. Okay, well, I could get a template or something, but I've looked at a few, and none of them really look like me." She just can't contain the urge.

"Stop. Just let the idea live and breathe for a minute."

"I'm not helping myself here, am I?" she says.

We both laugh. We have to turn off her mind and tune in to something else.

"Get up," I tell her.

"Okay, I'm up."

"What was that move you were describing to me that you did on a night dive? It was the one that resulted in a glitter trail of phosphorescence," I say recalling a previous conversation where she spoke of a magical scuba diving experience.

"Oh, that was a twirl; I was twirling underwater at night."

"Great. Are you wearing a headset right now?"

"Yes. I got a new one. It's wireless!"

"Fabulous. Start twirling."

There is a rush of air across the phone, followed by a stream of giggles—real laughter this time. The mind is gone; all that is left is my client's purest essence. Perfect. She returns to the phone and we begin talking again. Finally she's getting out three or four sentences about her website idea without adding a single *but*.

"That did it. I haven't heard one word from the Silencer in five minutes."

"I know," she says amazed. "It was so easy to shake it off."

Our time is coming to a close. "OK," I tell her, "here's your assignment should you choose to accept it: once an hour, no matter where you are, stop and twirl for a minute."

I don't know that she will stop doubting herself during the next two weeks between calls. Her mind is powerfully committed to this brand of disruption and distraction. I do think, though, that she can recognize it more clearly now and that she's discovered she has the power to stop it. She can use her body to interrupt and silence her mind when it is hurting her. Still, it can be hard to accept that the body is sometimes wiser than the mind. We return to the subject again a few weeks later.

I tell her, "Here's what's going on. It's been going on all year. Everything you've talked about, every conversation we've had has been marked by a deep resistance. I feel your resistance in my own muscles, it's that palpable. You have an answer for everything. Everything. There is never any time to allow something new to sink in. Your answer is already boomeranging back to me before what I've said can penetrate you."

"But I listen to everything you say, Holly, I do!" she protests.

"I don't care if you listen to me at all; you know that. What I'm struggling to point us toward is this: If you are boomeranging back, there is no chance to feel for resonance in the body. Your mind will not tell you that you are right; it's not convincing enough, even if it could allow you to be right. We have to find another way of determining what's right for you. My intuition says that your body is the place to go and that we need to find a way for you to feel the bodily resonance when true things are said.

There is a pause. Have I completely missed the mark? My own mind, too, always wants to doubt the wisdom of the body. I wait both myself and my client out.

Slowly she says, "I think you're right."

"Let's run a little experiment," I suggest. We take a subject about which her mind has sown nothing but doubt. I tell her to silence her mind completely and to make no response to my statements. I tell her I am going to say various things to her about this doubt-riddled subject and she is to say nothing except to share how it is resonating in her body.

I start with a statement that I believe is only partially true. We wait. She sits in silence.

"It feels sort of right, but sort of wrong." Bingo. The body barometer is working.

I make another statement, one that is plausible but ultimately false.

"That feels wrong. My mind is attracted to it, but my body isn't." Hallelujah!

I make a statement that affirms the strongest of her thoughts, the one I think she believes deep down. And we wait.

"When you say that, it's like hearing a perfect pitch on a tuning fork. Its rightness just reverberates all over my body." She is amazed to recognize this feeling within her. "And what do you feel as you're telling me this?"

"I'm so happy. I feel such a sense of relief, like there really is a way to *know*." I feel the same way.

"Great. Let's just call that done, shall we? Your body has confirmed it, so tell your mind the voting is closed on this issue."

"Yeah!" she says enthusiastically. I hear the lightness and rightness of it in her voice. This is the beauty of silencing thoughts. It allows for so much awareness of the space around oneself, both interior and exterior, and of the body's wisdom. Without the prolonged silence, I would never have seen the brutality of my own mind or my client's mind. Without the space provided by the silence, my client would have missed the experience of physical resonance, the feeling of witnessing her soul's truth spoken to her through her own body. Larry King, talk show host, once said, "I never learned anything while I was talking." Too right. Silence stills the mind like nothing else can, and this opens all sorts of gates on the path to enlightenment.

5

Holding with No Hands—Attachment

Life is difficult.

Life is difficult because of attachment,
because we crave satisfaction in ways
that are inherently dissatisfying.

The possibility of liberation from difficulties exists
for everyone.

The way to realize this liberation is ... by leading
a compassionate life of virtue, wisdom, and
meditation.

The Four Noble Truths[11]

The Four Noble Truths are the core of Buddhism. They are often recited with the term *suffering* in place of the word *difficulty*—that is, "Life is suffering," and so on. The translation I have used in the epigraph above is from *Awakening the Buddha Within,* by Lama Surya Das. The author makes the point, and I agree, that the more widely known translation is unnecessarily pessimistic and makes the Buddha's teaching less accessible. The Four Noble Truths are, he says, not pessimistic but in fact realistic; they merely describe how life *is* from a Buddhist view. [12]

Coaching provides an excellent opportunity to work with the concept that attachment is the cause of suffering. The Buddha observed that we cause our own difficulties by craving and clinging (being attached). We want, desire, and grasp after all sorts of things—money, jobs, people. Sometimes we get what we want from them only to find that we did not really want it, and suffering follows. Other times we do not get what we think we want from them, and suffering follows. Either way, grasping after money, jobs, and people—anything, really—causes suffering. When we release our attachments, "suffering falls away like drops of water falling from a flower."[13]

In the context of coaching it is often the case that the clinging causing the suffering centers on an idea or an intangible belief rather than on something tangible, such as money. Indeed many times the intangible is masked by the tangible, so it is important to keep looking behind the concrete thing for the idea or emotion that is fueling the attachment. Viewing this dilemma through the Buddhist lens can be powerful, for it reminds the coach and client of one very pragmatic route to alleviate the suffering: stopping the clinging itself. This chapter explores the beauty in the art of letting go.

***

My client has lost a client from her business. It seems like the end of everything, never mind the many other happy clients she is still serving. The fees of this one client are too necessary to the balance sheet.

"You sound like there is a massive weight pressing down on you."

"There is. It feels just like that."

I wonder what is next. The facts are the facts; a certain amount of money is needed at the end of the month and it is not going to be there. I don't know what she should do. I remind myself it is not my job to know, so I readjust the way I am listening to her. I realize that by allowing these fleeting thoughts to cross my mind, I am missing being with her.

She continues, despair creeping into her voice, "I just feel like I want to give up. I just want to collapse and give up." She is trying so very hard to pull herself together, to think clearly and deal with the situation, yet none of it is coming. What is coming is a wave of emotion and she is clinging to a twig called "keep it together." There is not enough twig here to make a life raft. I advise her to let go.

"Try lying down. Get all the way down on the floor and just give it up. Don't worry about being supported—the floor is there. And don't worry about getting up—I am here; I will get you up."

The sounds of fumbling and shuffling come across the

phone to me, and then it is done. I get down on my floor, too, across town. Though I have invited my client to take a leap through the body gate, I have my own struggle with it. It is never the first place I go, and it always feels foreign at first. Now, I am actually following my client into an on-the-floor free fall.

I hear tears come from the other end of the line. I brace myself, working consciously to relax. I still flinch at tears; I hate to hear suffering. I take a deep breath and again turn my focus on her and her tears. I find my place beside her. She speaks.

"Ohhhhh. Oh God, thank you." The relief is palpable. The tears flow, but stop faster than I expected. "Oh God, this feels great."

I smile. It does. My body has also released a mass of tension. I am tracking her now, allowing the floor to support us both, watching the arc of the moment float down. When it feels finished, I ask, "How do things look from here?"

"Possible. I'm staring up at the ceiling. It's a big blank. Anything is possible." It's not the most carefree pronouncement, but it is enough to bring her off the floor and back into the moment with something fresh.

***

My client and I are concluding our coaching engagement. It has happened sort of suddenly. We both knew the end was near, but weren't sure where or when until ten minutes into the telephone call.

"Wow, this is starting to sound like a completion call," I notice.

"It is, isn't it?"

"Yes, so let's go there and do that, since that's what's actually happening."

We shift gears and start talking more explicitly about the ground we've covered. As we talk and celebrate, I shine a light on the learning edge of each of her accomplishments during our time together, the place where she can continue looking on her own. She is happy with the coaching and where it has taken her. However, on my side, as I look at the edges, I see all the places I failed to push, to guide, to lead. I see my heart wrapping around the agenda she originally set for herself but did not attain. Of all the ways the dharma can guide me now, the one that calls to me is the concept of clinging. I listen to my client—she is not clinging to it; she is not suffering. In the same way I might guide a client to do, I now clasp my hands together, then release them. I do this over and over again until the physical act of locking and unlocking opens something inside my psyche and I find myself at ease. She is happy with our work. It is not my work. So who am I to be judging it? From time to time, whenever I realize I am clinging again, I simply lock and unlock my hands and rest. Slowly, I am less and less drawn back. The clinging is gone; the suffering stops.

***

My gym has a climbing wall. It is just to the left of the reception desk, and the second-floor balcony looks directly onto the top of it. I see it multiple times in any given trip to the gym, and I often think, *I should do another climb. I learned something so valuable on that last one.* When I finally schedule the climb, I resolve to get a jump on myself by forgetting about the goal from the start.

I am about a third of the way up again, looking for a handhold that doesn't seem apparent. I am moving quickly, testing this one and that, rejecting them, testing footholds, moving from side to side in the search for a good fit. There isn't any. Though I know it is useless to do so, I feel compelled to share my feelings. "They all suck," I call down, as if my trainer could, from where he stands, shift them around or make a good one appear. I hear a laugh back. In my humorless frame of mind, I dismiss it. I choose one and move. Now it's the next move. I feel a certain dogged energy rising in me. I am a persistent, some would say "stubborn," person, and right now I can feel it. Without realizing it, I begin to bring forward, almost reflexively, "my will." I cling to the idea that I can, with sheer force of will, override all obstacles. Part of me still believes that everything eventually yields to force and that in order to prevail, I simply have to summon the requisite amount of force. At this moment, suspended twenty feet above the floor by a couple of straps and a man I hardly know, I hold more tightly than ever to this belief.

I am two thirds of the way up now and seriously frustrated. I want to cry. Why did I do this? What can I possibly be learning? My hands are so tired. My clinging is both literal and figurative now. He calls up, "Holly, you don't have the strength in your hands. Loosen your grip." He's right. I relax my hands and to my surprise I don't fall off the rock. I move my attention into my legs. Better. Three more moves.

I call down weakly, "I'm tired."

"That's okay," he says cheerfully. "Just rest."

"What do you mean?" I ask.

"Just hang out in your seat. I've got you. I'm not in a hurry."

I had never thought of my harness as a "seat." In fact it had never actually occurred to me that I did not have to accomplish this climb in the least amount of time possible. I test him. I let my weight sink into my harness. It feels like a little chair swing, and I hang out and relax. I even swing a little. It's fun! As my sense of humor returns and my mood lightens, I realize this is exactly what I came here for, a refresher in nonattachment. I see more clearly now how I cling to the idea of force and I see the ways in which I constantly force myself to be productive. Still, I feel as if I should get moving for the sake of the man holding my rope. My inner critic is on fire screaming, *He isn't paid to hold you up in a swing.* But the calmer part of my mind replies, *Actually, he is.* I stay in my little seat a few minutes longer until a real desire to go on comes to me. Then I climb to the top.

6

Ruts, Patience, and Pushing

For everything there is a season,
And a time for every matter under heaven . . .
A time to break down and a time to build up . . .
A time to keep silence and a time to speak . . . .

Ecclesiastes 3:1–8

One thing coaches and clients tend to become attached to is a preference for forward motion. It is hard not to. Coaches are naturally drawn to forward motion, because they are, by and large, "doers." And this is why clients are generally drawn to them. Clients want change and forward motion in their lives, so they seek out an extra pair of hands to help shove the boat into the water, so to speak. Sometimes, however, this movement proves elusive. And if the coach and the client cling to their love of forward motion, or exacerbate any aversion to slow motion or stillness, suffering will follow. What to do then? Buddhism gives more than one answer here. There are times when one must acknowledge reality as it is and wait for the natural change in the current to set the boat on its way. But then there are other times when one must emphasize determination and remind the client of the impermanence of everything, especially that of their own lives, so the boat does not become beached and stuck. This chapter explores both of those ideas.

All of us are in transition all the time. You are in a transition this very moment, although you probably don't realize it. For example, you are reading this now, but at some point you will stop reading and start focusing elsewhere. And then at some other point you will choose, commit, and transition into doing something else. Clients, too, are in transition all the time, and they will seek out coaching, either consciously or unconsciously, as a way to help make sense of whatever part of the cycle they are in. Most come to coaching holding fast to their attachment to forward motion. Here is where an aware coach can make a profound difference.

Most people in Western cultures think of transition as being something that starts at point A and moves in a straight line along specific steps to point B, where the socially acceptable goal is waiting with fulfillment, happiness, and a gold watch. There is a great deal of social science research that suggests the cycle of transition is better conceived of as a circle, one that undulates in sync with the cycles of nature, similar to the seasons of the year or the passing of the day.[14]

The seasons are a particularly useful metaphor for describing the cycle of change. As with the seasons, there are four stages in the cycle. "Fall" is the stage where many coaches and clients first meet. Here, change is in the air though the form of the next thing is as yet unknown. In the next stage, "Winter," the client often goes into deep introspection. Unfortunately this is where many coaches and clients give up, since the pace usually slows down dramatically. The next stage, "Spring" is marked by a surge of ideas about the new potential form, and here is where coaches and clients can often best enjoy their collaboration. The cycle completes itself with "Summer," where the idea, which now has a concrete form, is brought into manifestation.

The most important thing for coaches and clients to understand is that Fall and Winter are not seasons that require action. Rather, these phases are about going inside and being with the endings of things. They are the seasons of recollection, appreciation of things let go, and are for rest and rejuvenation. Whatever forward motion Fall and Winter have may be entirely internal and it usually happens slowly. According to Carol Vecchio, executive director for Centerpoint Institute for LifeWork Renewal, the average time spent cycling through these phases is five years. In other words, a person contemplating a career change, for example, is thinking about it, on average, for five years before she actually takes action. For that reason coaching, with its focus on action, can put both the coach and the client in a paradoxical position. On the one hand, it is true that there are times when, especially in Fall and Winter, all the shoving in the world cannot budge the boat from the shore. On the other hand, honoring and respecting the cycle and its timing is not a passive exercise, and even in these seasons where external action is generally not recommended, clients can use coaching to remain accountable and focused on the internal tasks at hand. The key for coaches working with Fall and Winter clients is to commit to growth over action, to press on in the service of growth, and to recognize that, regardless of where the client is in the cycle, the tide will rise again and the boat will make its way back to the water.

**

My client is in transition around two of the dominant areas of her life, her relationship and her job. We talk about the cycle of transition and check all three markers—energy, emotional content, and vision—with respect to each area. About the major areas of her life, the answers are the same. Energetically, she spikes up and down. Some days it all seems fine and doable, while other days it's the pits. Sometimes she goes for several days feeling flat and numb. None of it feels good. Emotionally, she is in turmoil. It feels to her like both of these major areas are on a general downswing and are moving toward some kind of an ending, but she has not yet decided to actually leave any of it behind. She tells herself that what she needs is a vacation from the job, but we both know she'll be back to this point of frustration in a week or less. Some days she's angry at someone, other days she's depressed. When we talk about a vision for the future, she is able to articulate what a good future would look like, but the steps between her and the realization of that vision are invisible to her. We can both see that the relationship and the job, in particular, are headed for some sort of change because she finds neither one satisfying.

I suggest she think of this being Fall in these two life areas. Just as the leaves turn color, die, and fall from the trees, aspects of her life, too, are in the process of withering and dying. In this season it is not uncommon to see a client's emotional experience mirroring the five stages of grief identified by Elisabeth Kűbler-Ross. First there is denial ("He's really a good person aside from all the cheating"); then anger ("Why is this happening to me?"); then bargaining ("I just need a vacation"); then depression ("I can't get out of bed this morning") and finally acceptance ("I don't know what I'm going to do, but it won't be this!").[15]

Energetically my client is going inward, which is why she has sought out a coach, though she might not say so explicitly. Like most fast-paced, successful people, she is very skilled at many of the exterior aspects of her life, but making sense of the interior is more of a challenge for her. She is slowing down and bumping along an arc that is generally moving downward. This is uncomfortable for most people and this is why people seek out coaches at this time: we all want company in this unsettling territory. My client's sense of vision about where she is going and what she really wants is, like most Fall clients, unclear. She knows it is not "this," but she is not sure how to make her way toward "that." She isn't even sure she is ready to end the relationship or quit her job. She wants to know what is ahead. We talk about the next phase, about Winter and its emphasis on rest, rejuvenation, and gathering energy. "Spell it out for me," she demands.

We talk about introspection, gathering energy internally, rejuvenating, and finding the essence of what is to come next. I remind her that even if it looks on the surface as if all is dead, important changes are in fact going on underneath, changes that can only be revealed in due time, during the Spring. During the Winter phase clients can sometimes feel very stuck, depressed, lost, and confused, and energetically they may appear stagnant or still. At the other extreme are the clients who are exuberantly experiencing themselves as liberated from the shackles of the past.

Clients who are wintering well are mobilizing their energies by doing things to rejuvenate themselves. They might be knitting furiously, even after a ten-year hiatus, making baby booties in every color and four sizes, even though they don't actually have a baby on the way. Or they might be reading book after book, cooking great meals, catching up on their sleep, completing crossword puzzles, traveling, or engaging in sports. One Winter client I had found it deeply restorative to read thought-provoking works. My job, in fact, was to stop her from trying to find clients and building her business and to hold her accountable to her commitment to sit down and read as voraciously as her heart desired. From her seemingly endless reading came a collection of ideas that formed into a business some months later. Without her Winter "vacation," this might not have happened.

This is, in fact, how Joseph Campbell came into his own as the preeminent thinker and writer on the role of myth in our culture. For five years he engaged in independent study on a wide variety of subjects, reading up to nine hours each day about everything from Sanskrit to modern art. Modern society has little patience for this part of the cycle because it is not about making money or being part of the larger world's plan. But once the client is replenished, an essence begins to come forward, a feeling of purpose or concern or direction will start forming around something. When that essence is known and ready to bud, Winter is over and Spring is at hand.

I offer my client a couple of possible scenarios: A week-long silent Buddhist retreat on Mount Shasta. A commitment to eat lunch alone every day for a month and do nothing but notice what her heart is drawn to. An agreement to quit her job and wander through the countryside of her favorite state by car, stopping where and when she wants.

"Quit my job? Without another one?" she asks incredulously.

"That's one scenario," I say. She has the resources to transition without a job and her present situation is so toxic, welfare would honestly be a better option.

"I've never done that. Not in forty-eight years." She is baffled by the idea. "I've never not worked for more than two weeks at a time."

"What would rejuvenate you?"

She immediately thinks of her usual stimulants. She moves very fast, she's never done anything but move fast, and she thinks this is the only way to reinvigorate herself. I can tell, though, that her soul wants something different. Her soul wants a rest. It is apparent in the way she questioned the idea of just quitting.

We talk some more about the seasons. "How does Winter end?" she asks.

"Well, after a person replenishes herself, the essence of what is truly wanted will start to emerge. The emotional feel of your life will change; the energy becomes more stable and starts to rise. It's as natural as the trees beginning to bud, or the ice beginning to melt."

"What if it doesn't?"

"You are part of nature. Your body is an organic entity that is tuned to the cycles of the environment and the seasons. The nature of life is to change. All of this means that transition is inevitable."

I can sense that she has sat back in her chair. I can feel her taking this in. She is quiet.

"What are you feeling as we talk about the possibility of ending these things and committing to introspection?" I ask.

"I don't think I can do it."

We talk more about the ways it could go—winter in Buffalo or winter in Bermuda? Each has its own charm, but let's not kid anyone; Bermuda beats Buffalo. We begin talking about how one creates a Bermuda-like Winter and what one might do while there. The value of Winter begins to grow on her.

"God, you know, I think I really would love to be doing nothing. I mean it, nothing." She is contemplating with wonder the idea of getting up at ten o'clock in the morning, lounging around, reading the paper, and seeing, maybe for the first time as an adult, what interests her. And nothing else.

"Simply doing nothing might be the best thing in the world. For you that would really be quite an accomplishment." We laugh. The irony is not lost on either of us. This is a goal-oriented person, so the word accomplishment has made the idea attractive the way nothing else can. But in the end she still cannot commit to endings. The idea of Winter, while alluring, is too foreign, too risky to accept. She decides to stay where she is, neither moving nor introspecting, and the coaching terminates shortly thereafter.

The concept of forward motion, however, is paradoxical in nature, because there is another side to it that is equally valid, and that perspective likewise finds support in the Buddhist teaching about impermanence. The other perspective on this (and there are surely more than these two) is that there are times, even in the slow seasons, where a good strong push is needed and welcome. Buddhism teaches us to embrace the fact that we are all going to die, not for morbid reasons, but rather so that we can get serious about really living. Sometimes just realizing that our lives are very short is all a person needs to catalyze motion. Clinging to either perspective too tightly does not serve either the coach or the client well. The better practice, I think, is to hold them both and try to determine in each moment where it is best to stand. Since both are sound, no one can ever really be "wrong."

***

It is February 2006 and I am in the midst of a mini-Winter myself. I am hibernating in Dunedin, New Zealand, a town of about 150,000 people. I am very close to the South Pole right now, both literally and figuratively; I am in a funk. On the outside I appear to be stagnant. My clientele is gradually falling off and I am not doing anything to replenish the pipeline. I have not made any friends to speak of in our new home. I am, however, engaged in the leadership program, and massive internal restructuring is occurring in me just beneath the surface. I start to feel quite restless. It is as though the ice of my Winter is about to thaw, yet I still have six months to go, maybe longer, before leaving New Zealand. I sense that I am in a holding pattern, but I am not aware of my seasonal position.

"It's going to be a long six months," I tell my coach dolefully.

He leaps on this and tries a good, hard shove. He knows I have been struggling to get my head above water for some time and he has been patiently letting me do my own work. Today he jumps in with more direction than usual.

"You *could* make this the most productive, creative six months of your life. You could use the time to create a plan for the life you want when you get home. You could write a whole book."

"It's true," I agree blandly. He is right, but I am not moved.

"What if this was the last six months of your life?" he asks. "What would you be doing?"

I think of one of the co-leaders of my leadership program. She has Stage IV cancer. Although she looks radiant and healthy, the cancer is metastasizing at an alarming rate, and I have wondered more than once if she will make it to the end of the program, which is next month. I consider my coach's question with this in the back of my mind.

What would I do if I only had six months to live? Travel madly? No. I love to travel, but that would not be my choice. Visit all those "loose end" people and try to tie up the ragged edges of relationships past? No. I'd love to have it all neat and tidy, but as I consider the question, I realize there isn't much left undone, and the rest I don't really care about. Eat as much dessert as I want? Well, yes. I would not limit my consumption of cheesecake the way I do now.

"No question: the book. I'd just tell everyone to jump off a bridge, that I'm busy, I'm writing." I hear myself say. In my mind, I add, *Okay, so act like it.* It's the kick in the pants I need. Suddenly the book starts writing itself. In two months' time I have seventy pages done. At the rate I'm going, it *will* have been the most productive six months of my life.

There I was in my Winter funk. Some would have said, "Let her be, she'll move when she's ready." But sometimes we don't always know we're ready. The season is changing, but we're as aware of this as a groundhog that hasn't yet surfaced to check for its shadow. This demonstrates the power of the coaching sangha. You can always count on someone to at least try to shove that wheel, and sometimes the touch of a human hand and the knowledge that someone cares enough to try may be enough to get you going.

In the cycle of transition, Spring begins when the essence of what is next reveals itself and it's time to find forms to match it. For example, if a person is in transition around his job, Spring may be the time when it becomes clear that the right job for him must involve numbers, but he isn't certain whether this means accounting, teaching math, or something else entirely. Spring is a time of exploration to find the form in which the client's new essence can thrive. Energetically, clients in this phase tend to be more alive, more positive, and more consistent with respect to finding the new form. Emotionally, there is a sense of optimism, tempered by the anxiety of wanting to choose the "right" thing or the sense of needing to find it quickly. With respect to vision, clients in this season become increasingly concrete. What starts as an essence will turn into a form, and when it does, the next phase—Summer—begins.

***

I am working with my coach in the Spring season now. I know that I need work which makes use of my personality and my people skills and I know that I need some sort of creative outlet. I am exploring a myriad of options for creating a new career: real estate, web design, interior design, coaching and a few others, which change from time to time depending on my mood. When I'm in a pessimistic frame of mind, I consider some version of lawyering again; when I am thinking optimistically, something creative and funky always surfaces. My impatience is constantly flaring up, like an aching joint that responds to weather changes.

"I just need to pick one and get on with it," I tell her.

"What will happen if you do?"

"Well, I'll get going and I'll either be happy or I won't."

"And if you're not happy, what will you do?"

"Knowing me, I'll gut it out for five more years before I admit I screwed up," I say, laughing at the prospect of me being me.

"Which would you rather waste, three more weeks or five years?" she asks sweetly. I laugh. She is right. Better to slow down and take the time now than to race forward and have to take the time later.

***

Summer is the season of high energy. The vision has become clear and the client is acting to realize it. Emotionally, clients feel a sense of purpose, direction, and commitment. It is a gratifying time for most people. Energetically, Summer clients tend to be powerhouses. They are working hard, often too hard, consumed by their passion and desire to attain the goal. The vision is not in doubt in the Summer phase; if it ever gets a little dim, it's usually a matter of fine-tuning some aspect of it rather than going for a wholesale switch. No longer is forward motion an issue; it is the pace of the motion that poses challenges now. Fortunately, the practices of Buddhism naturally speak to the problems associated with life lived at an accelerated speed.

***

My client is in Summer. She is clearly committed to losing weight and finding a new job working in the hospitality industry. She is being proactive and making things happen. She is a busy person, with stressful work. Our coaching centers around accountability, brainstorming, and strategizing, and it keeps pace with her life; together we move fast, even on the phone. She calls me after she's through with work one night, and for the first time she sounds tired. She starts with a yawn.

"Oh, God, sorry," she says, excusing herself.

"No need. I'm glad to know where you are tonight; it sounds like you're on 'slow.'"

She laughs. "Yeah, more like 'no, go.'"

"Do you want to reschedule this call?"

"No, no."

"Okay. So tell me what you're noticing right now," I ask, slowing my voice and dropping my own energy down.

"Hmmm. A picture. It's hanging on my wall. It's a painting, actually. It's been there for God knows how long, and this is the first time I'm really looking at it."

"What does that make you aware of?"

"Jesus, I wonder what else has been sitting right in front of me that I haven't noticed. It's a really pretty painting."

"What is the effect of looking at it?"

"I feel sort of peaceful. And I shouldn't. It has not been a peaceful sort of day."

She starts to launch into a description of her day, at a higher speed, more typical of her usual pace, but I cut her off.

"Stay with the painting," I say quietly.

I can hear her speed diminishing on the other end of the line.

"Good idea," she says after a moment.

"What's come up now?"

"I really like that pink. It's a sunset and the pink is so lovely." She almost sounds wistful.

"What is pink to you?"

"Innocent, soft, kid, gentle. It's a break. Like a little place to rest."

"Mmmm. Have you ever meditated?"

"No. I mean, I've heard of it, I kind of know what it is, but I haven't ever tried it."

"We could do a few minutes right now, just to see what it's like to stay with this sort of pace, if you want."

"Okay, sure."

"Okay, so just stay with your painting and turn off your mind. Focus on your breathing and let the thoughts drift away. They'll pop up, but just put your focus back on your breathing. You can count silently if that will help you. I'll stop you at two minutes." I let the second hand find a number and say, "Begin."

We sit in silence for two minutes. I tell her it's time, and then ask, "What's there now?"

"It seemed like a long time. It's hard to believe that was really only two minutes. It was weird. But nice. I mean, as long as I didn't think about what I am doing or what is Holly thinking, it was fine."

"What's there now?" She is quiet. She laughs weakly and says, "I'm thinking there is so little that is soft in my world." This is not an overstatement. I have been to her office and I know the nature of her work.

She forces herself to brighten, as is her habit, and says, "I really like that pink. More pink."

"What would it be like to take pink to work?"

"I think it would nice. I think it would make it easier to be there while I'm looking for a job."

"What is the sensation of pink?"

"It's slowing down. It's just being still for a minute and knowing the world is not going to cave in."

We go on this way. It is the slowest, most quiet call I have ever had with a client, and one of the loveliest. We both emerge from it refreshed and notice how good it was for our coaching relationship to slow down too. With two minutes of the ancient practice of meditation we have put in check one of the most common problems of the action seasons: burnout. As with the other seasons, coaching provides a great context for exploring common modern questions with timeless Buddhist answers.

7

Mirrors—A Look at Samsara

Insanity: doing the same things over and over again
expecting different results.

Albert Einstein

*S*amsara is a Sanskrit term with many translations, one of which is "conditioned existence." Samsara or conditioned existence refers to our human tendency to create and perpetuate suffering for ourselves by doing the same fruitless things over and over again—things such as choosing the same types of unsatisfying romantic partners, working for the same overbearing boss in four different jobs, or having the same unproductive conversations with our children.

Here, too, awareness is the key to finding an answer, and coaching can provide a unique place to develop that awareness. Most people do not knowingly choose to do painful things to themselves. They make those choices because they do not see what they are doing. They look at things and fail to see the parallels between their past and present situations. Coaches can help clients break through samsara if they themselves are aware of the mirroring dynamic that inevitably emerges within the coaching relationship.

***

I have been pacing around, wondering if I should bring up the topic of my marriage in this coaching call. It is such a private area and I have never approached this part of my life with my coach. When he and I came together, we did so by walking through the door called "My Book," so we are not supposed to be in the room marked "My Marriage," but that is where I am today. I need to bounce ideas off someone who doesn't know and love my husband, like all my friends do. I decide to plunge in and to take my coach with me. Who knows what we'll see with two pairs of eyes? Now I am almost eager to get in there and look around. Because my coach is currently traveling I am waiting for a call from him rather than placing it myself.

It is 10:10. Now 10:30. Now 10:40. I learn later we have simply bollixed up the half-a-planet time difference, but right now it is well past our appointed time and I am too let down to pick up the phone. A storm of emotions surges through me, and I decide to sit down and write about it. This is my version of a rosary. Others take beads in hand to sift through their worries and find guidance; I tap keys. This is my spiritual ritual, and like those who use rosaries, I find access to something higher, more pure and clear.

As I write, I see parallels between my feelings about my coach and those I have with my husband. In both relationships I feel a coolness and distance with the other person, which I don't understand and don't like. In both situations I want so much to bridge the gap, but I haven't a clue how to go about it. In both, there are things I want so much to talk about, but when I marshal the courage to do so, the other person just doesn't seem to be available. By the time I am finished writing, it is almost as if these two important people in my life have become interchangeable. But I am not in love with my coach, so what's going on here?

***

My client and I are on the phone unexpectedly early. I needed to move the time of the appointment up by half an hour, and since she was willing and able to do it, we're chatting now. Suddenly I hear an alarm clock go off in the background at her end.

"What's that?" I ask.

I can "hear" her blushing. "Oh, I always set my alarm before our calls, to get myself together before we talk."

"As in 'prepare'?" I ask. I am surprised, and I can't mask these things.

"Yeah." She laughs a bit, picking up on my shock. "I have to think about what I am going to say."

"What's that about?"

"I guess I don't want to disappoint you, you know, by showing up unprepared."

I rifle through my memory bank, searching for any misstep I may have made in the past. I have worked with this woman for too long for her to be thinking such things. Now I start doing to myself what she does all the time to herself—"shoulding." *I should have known she was hiding. I should have made the space more open.* I snap my attention away from myself and focus on the fact that some part of her has been putting on an act for me.

"Who else are you showing up for like this?"

She thinks about it for a moment and admits, "Just about everyone."

"How's it working for you?"

She chuckles like a child caught with her mother's lipstick. She's been using it to create a certain look, but now she is exposed.

"Tell me more."

"It's stressful. I'm never really myself. And that's tiring."

I am aching inside. How have I failed to create that space for her, I wonder? This is the one place she is supposed to be able to feel completely herself. What's going on here?

***

In both circumstances the mirroring dynamic has come into play. Because of the nature of the coaching relationship, coaches invariably reflect back to clients their samsaric condition and their repetitive choices that create disharmony. In that frustrating moment between my coach and me when he didn't call, my painful feelings about my husband were inadvertently reflected back to me. In the same way, I became a mirror for my client, reflecting back to her the pattern of pleasing others that was exhausting her. In both instances, the client brought her seemingly unrelated personal issues into the coaching relationship. When the coach and client recognize the inevitability of this, there is a unique opportunity to end one of the many unconscious patterns of which samsara is composed.

In most of the other ways in which our hidden "scripts" play themselves out in our lives, we are too attached to be able to see what we are doing, and the other people (my husband, in my case; everyone else, in my client's) have no idea what is going on for us. And even if they do, they lack the objectivity to step aside and point out to us what's going on. They, too, are attached to their role play and the outcome. A coach without an agenda, on the other hand, can do an amazing service for his or her client by pointing out this mirroring effect and simply being curious about it.

Once the mirror has been recognized, it can still be tricky to understand what's really going on. The coach-client relationship has a certain objectivity, but it is still a relationship between two human beings, and as such, when difficult feelings come up, it's not always clear whether there's something truly interpersonal going on or if it's simply a reflection of the client's own unresolved issues. It may be both. My coach and I looked at the mirror together and I decided to explore my samsara via my relationship with him rather than talking about my relationship with my husband. My client opted to examine her desire to please others at the expense of her authenticity by examining a relationship with another person in her life rather than look at the dynamic in relation to me. My coach and I worked with the "mirror" by talking about the coolness between us, about the silent spots in our dialogue, and about my genuine desire to be closer. And as we did so, he encouraged me to be with him as I wished I could be with my husband. Exercising exquisite self-management, he let me use him to practice a new way of being. I, too, allowed my client to practice on me by role-playing, more authentic ways of being with people even when she felt the need to please them.

Though the mirror phenomenon can be puzzling at the time, if either person in the relationship can recognize the dynamic as it is emerging, there is a unique and beautiful opportunity to assist the client in transcending his or her samsara and move toward both fulfillment and enlightenment. The coaching sangha can provide a place where a client can cultivate awareness about choices and behavior and can practice new ways of being with safety, confidentiality, and no judgment. It is like standing in front of the bathroom mirror practicing a speech. One can fumble, get it wrong, and start over ten times, but only so long as both the coach and the client understand that the mirror dynamic is in play and that the coaching is being used for that purpose. This is an excellent way to interrupt the cycle of samsara, experiment with new strategies, and cultivate new awareness until both sanity and peace are restored.

8

Going Off the Map, Finding the Way

Does one really have to fret about enlightenment?
No matter what road I travel, I'm going home.

Shinso, 15ᵗʰ c. Japanese poet

You are walking down a dimly lit corridor in a restaurant, on the way to the restroom. You reach the little vestibule where two doors present themselves. They are clearly marked. You reach for the appropriate door, thrust it open, and stride in like you own the place, only to find three shocked people of the opposite sex turning to look at you. You back out of the restroom, almost tripping over your own feet, and stare at the door incredulously. How can this be? You look at the signage again. You could swear it said something different when you looked at it the first time.

This is how it is in coaching. At the beginning of the work, client and coach talk about focal points for the coaching—the "Why are you here?" conversation. The client comes up with three or four answers to this question, and you agree to help her or him to explore those territories. You have, in essence, created a map of where this is going. You begin the coaching, pushing open the doors marked "My Lousy Job" and "My Slacker Work Team," only to find you are somewhere else completely. Before you know it, the room marked "My Lousy Job" has become "My Inability to Say No," and it's more than a single room, it's an entire wing of the house.

You are now off the map. Congratulations! Going off the map usually means you have arrived in exactly the right place. One of the key tools for finding your way when you are off the map, either emotionally or cognitively, can be found in the Buddhist principle of nonjudgment.

In Buddhism, and in coaching, it becomes less important to decide whether an experience is "good" or "bad" than to recognize that one is slipping into a dualistic perspective. The term *dualistic* has to do with seeing things according to opposite poles of good/bad, right/wrong, and it's the way most of us think most of the time, although we do so unconsciously. A coach who recognizes the poison of dualism can lead a client into a more constructive "middle way"[16] by modeling a different way of thinking. For example, a client may be wondering, "Should I be assertive or detached in this situation?" An alert coach can reframe this for the client as "What is needed from me here?" or "What stance is consistent with my innately perfect self?" If we follow the Buddhist rule and consistently strive to see the naked reality of the situation rather than making judgments and assigning labels of "good" or "bad," we can let go of our maps and simply create a new path from wherever we stand at the moment, moving forward from there in the best way possible. Though it is sometimes difficult to do this, the unexpected places we go are so wondrous and rich that they are worth any concerns or stumbling blocks we may encounter along the way.

***

My client and I have been working on her career shift for several months now. Within a few sessions of beginning our work, it quickly becomes apparent that she has an unrequited love of the natural sciences. She had thought that perhaps she could get close enough to it by choosing patent law as a specialty, but so far all she's gotten is a life as a frustrated lawyer. She is sure it's not just the fact that she's with a start-up company that cannot manage its own growth or decide how to include her in its structure; it is more than that, she says. She wants to get away from practicing law. And so we set out, exploring ways that she can fulfill her love of science and put food on the table at the same time. Finally she admits that her longtime fantasy has been to practice medicine. Over several months she builds up the courage to investigate completely changing course. We find the path littered with obstacles, both real and imaginary. We take them on, one at a time, and before long she commits to the idea of going to medical school. She signs up for the MCAT review course and figures out when she will take the entrance exam and how she will pay for it. It's happening.

We meet several months later at the coffee shop on the corner, both of us foregoing the shop's legendary cupcakes, and take our drinks to the park a block away. We lounge on a patch of dry grass, taking in the just-warm-enough sun of the Seattle spring. We joke with each other and catch up. Finally I turn to her and say, "Tell me again." She looks down, then off to the side, then finally at me. She had said in our last phone conversation that she'd decided not to go to medical school after all. I'd said, "Let's get together."

"I've thought about it, Holly," she says, "I really have. And I still feel the same as I did on the phone last week. I don't want to go after all." She begins twirling her paper coffee cup between her hands like a pot being opened up on a potter's wheel, rhythmically, steadily. "I can hardly believe it myself, after all the work we've done on it."

I am not convinced, but I notice that she sounds convinced. "What has brought you to this point?"

"It was something I heard Dr. Phil say," she says in a tone that conveys her own disbelief that she is buying into the conclusions of a maverick psychologist turned daytime talk show host. "He was talking to a woman who claimed to really want and need a new car, but she could not afford it at all. She'd been convinced that she had to have the car, so he asked her to imagine having the car and how she would feel. Then he said, 'Go find that same feeling somewhere else, somewhere that isn't going to bankrupt you.' And I've just been thinking, What is the feeling that's really under med school and how could I get that feeling without doing this to myself?"

It's a good question. Changing directions at this point in her life and going to medical school would have entailed a huge sacrifice for her, given the present circumstances of her life. But I hardly hear the words, so closely am I watching her energy to see if I can notice any signs of resignation or doubt in her about this change in her plans—but there are none to be found. We talk a bit more, and I am satisfied that my obligation to keep her pointing "North" toward her true self does not include pressing her any further on this. This *is* the truth; at least it is the truth of this moment. Still, there is an air of sadness.

I struggle with the fact that a year's work seems to have gone down the drain, because quietly, without even noticing it, I am judging our new place on the map. We are far from where we started, her dissatisfaction with the "lousy job" is a dim signpost in the distance, and there is a part of me that has not yet adjusted. Then I realize that we're both sad. It's something that is here in the present for both of us. So I unstick myself from my own feelings and get curious about it.

"What do you make of the fact that we've been

committed to this for almost a year and now you're dropping it?" I ask.

"I don't know," she says. "I know that this hasn't been a waste of time. There was a purpose in it. But I don't know what to say right now."

We pass the disbelief back and forth a few more moments, and then it hits me. We both thought the door was marked "Medical School," but as I stand here on the outside looking back at it, I realize it had changed once we'd gone inside. The room had transformed into "Permission and Choice," and taking the intention to go to medical school seriously became the access point to develop this in her life. The proof that she was successful in this is that now she is allowing herself to choose again, even though the choice is "no."

In retrospect, I see that my client was not ready to make the major shift of leaving her career. From a seasonal perspective, she was just beginning to work through the average time of a situation in transition. I, too, felt this way after practicing law for two and a half years. I knew I had chosen incorrectly for myself, but I was not ready to leave the profession. It took me five more years to make my way to the next point in the cycle of transition, and my guess is she will revisit her desire to be something other than a lawyer. When she does, however, she will have an advantage, in that she spent this time cultivating a new facet to her character that will serve her well when the time is ripe. She knows how to allow herself permission and she knows how to stand by her heart's choice.

***

My client of three months has come to the coaching call intending to quit. "I think you're great and it's been good to have someone to talk with, but I just think it's probably best if I don't go on with the coaching," she says.

She, too, had come to me three months earlier and pointed at a door marked "My Lousy Job." We set off, map in hand, in search of her next job, and now here we are at a dead end. There was no dead end on the map when we started our trip. How have we ended up here? I accept the fact that this is my last call with her as soon as she says so. I learned early on not to grasp after clients; that is a truly painful attachment. But there is something more to say here. There is a reality that neither of us is acknowledging. My heart begins to race, not because I am being nicely fired but rather because I know it is time to acknowledge an unpleasant fact. I know now why we have wandered into this dead end; what's coming next needs to happen.

"You're whining."

"I am?" she says, surprised. I don't know if she is surprised that I said it or surprised that she may in fact be whining.

"Yep. You have one voice that comes out when you're in your strong, grounded future-self place and really know what you're talking about. And then there's this one where you do all your whining." I make a mental note that being fired up front is very liberating. I wonder if I should have all my clients fire me at the beginning, or if I should just fire myself? I press on.

"Get into your future self," I tell her.

There is a pause. Then, "Okay." Even that sounds different. Her voice is about an octave deeper, no air in it and a lot of muscle.

"Okay, great. Now tell me you're quitting and stay in that voice."

She starts to say it again, but it just won't come out.

"See? That wasn't really you talking. If you want to quit, that's fine, but I have to know that it's really you—your real, strong self—that wants to quit, not your whiner. That one is always going to want to quit. What else do you feel like quitting?" We go on and finish the call, talking about something else altogether. At the end I ask her if she's coming back or not.

"Yes. I'm coming back," she says in her real voice. We have found another path as a result of being in this off-the-map place. We work together for another year, and in that time she anchors herself to this strong self and almost doubles her pay, then moves to a new city and begins her second career.

In the midst of all this, she takes me off the map again. This time we find ourselves talking about her boyfriend.

He wasn't even mentioned in the "Why are you here?" conversation. Definitely not on the map I had. She circles around the fact that he should be what she wants, and he is not. *What a pity, I think; he's cute, smart, and clearly adores her.* I catch myself. I am judging. I see myself thinking he is right for her. I back off.

"I guess part of the problem is that there is someone else," she says evenly, as if the slightest move will set her in the path of an avalanche. "I work with him," she continues. "He is much older than me, and he's separated but not divorced. I wasn't going to talk to you about him, but I told a friend about the coaching and she said I should."

The number of doors I have to bypass are too numerous to count. I leave the "Should" door unopened; I bypass the man's ambiguous marital status, his age, their proximity at work. The fact that she is for the first time revealing his existence is calling, so I respond to that instead. My client has been talking about her boyfriend for three months, with no mention of this other man. She is such an honest person and we have such a good connection that I am a bit stunned to realize she has not told me the complete, unvarnished truth. Since I can't really think my way out of being stunned, I abandon my logical mind and turn 180 degrees in the other direction, toward my heart.

"I'm so glad you finally told me. No wonder we were going around in circles about your boyfriend."

She chuckles. "Yeah, I guess that wasn't too smart."

I see she is starting to judge herself, so I begin to work to neutralize it. "I wouldn't call it 'smart' or 'dumb'; it's human. You had to decide if you could trust me."

We talk about her feelings for the boyfriend and compare them to those for the other man, exploring them all for texture, intensity, and resonance. After really looking at her feelings, she comes to the conclusion that she cannot continue a relationship where she is feeling flat. She is leaving the boyfriend. "I expected you to think I was a horrible person, totally immoral," she says, wondering why I have not condemned her.

It is my turn to stand in the line of the oncoming avalanche. I honestly think no less of her as a person, but the truth is that I can't think of a romantic scenario less promising than the one she has described. I want to shield her from disappointment the way a big sister might. But I am not her big sister, I am her coach, and she is naturally creative, resourceful, and whole, I remind myself. I recall reading about a Buddhist lama's response to a practitioner who'd admitted using mind-altering drugs, contrary to the teachings of Buddhism. Rather than condemn the person, the lama used it as an opportunity to teach a different dharma lesson, about attachment: "If you see anything beautiful [while using hallucinogens], don't cling to it; if you see anything ugly, don't cling to it; whatever the mind produces, don't cling to it."[17] This story, combined with my own experiences as a client, helps me to respond here.

I tell her, "We have all stood in those shoes in one way or another. It is not my job to tell you your shoes are awful. My job is to ask how well you think they fit. If we had spent our time condemning your choice in shoes, I'm not sure we would have gotten around to the real truth, which is this: The ones you were wearing don't fit. We'll see how these others feel after you walk around in them for a while." I know that the best service I can provide for my client in this moment is to help her to know her own heart. I know that her internal compass will not allow her to be in this situation for very long. And I know that my job is to keep pointing her toward her true self. It will all come together in due course. And it does. Ultimately she discards the second pair of shoes as well; they are not suited for the road she is walking either.

***

My husband and I are in Hawaii at Volcanoes National Park. We are driving on the main road, headed for a five-square-mile area of lava. We arrive at the visitors' outpost and read about the lava on the fact boards. I read that people are advised not to go beyond a certain point because quickly changing winds can leave one in the wake of toxic, volcanic gases. I don't need to read any more. I am content to view the peculiar, hardened lava field from the safety of the building. Predictably, my husband begins exploring beyond the immediate area. "I'm just going out to that edge over there." He trots off to a boundary marker. I reluctantly follow.

The next thing I know we are the only two people to be seen; we are surrounded by the hardened black lava, above us the open sky. Periodically we come upon a Park Service sign that suggests now would be a good time to turn back. And on we go. Finally we arrive at a sign that says, in no uncertain terms, Go Back. Not One Step Further. He takes the binoculars and ventures on a few feet more. I remain fixed, agitated, and annoyed.

A few moments later he begins gesturing madly for me to come out. It's only a little farther. I go. I am so far beyond the safety of the gas-free building that another few steps aren't going to make a difference. Going beyond the markers is no longer a "good" or a "bad" thing. It's just what we are doing. He hands me the binoculars and points to the horizon. I fumble for a few minutes and then I see it, a pulsing, live river of orange and red molten lava, pouring forth passionately, spilling into the ocean. As it slides into the water, a zipper of steam rises above it. It is one of the most amazing things I have ever seen. I am transfixed by the lava river. I could stand here all day. I am watching the earth regenerate itself before my very eyes.

As German philosopher Martin Buber said, "All journeys have secret destinations of which the traveler is unaware." This is especially true of the journey taken by coaches and clients. Most of the life-changing, glorious sights are off the map. You only find them by chance and after taking some risks. They are always worth it, although you must be a little adventurous and somewhat imprudent to find them. But if you can see the terrain for what it is, rather than what you expected, the way will unfold before you.

9
The Question of Desire

All great truths begin as blasphemies.

George Bernard Shaw

According to Buddhism, the fires of desire and the disquiet they arouse are invariably consuming and cause a great deal of suffering. Buddhists believe extinguishing desire is the prerequisite to achieving nirvana, the state of bliss where one's attachment to the ego dissolves and the individual becomes one with everything and at peace with everything.

This poses a difficulty for Western seekers of the modern era and the coaching relationship puts a fine point on this difficulty. This industry is, like so much of modern industry, predicated on wish fulfillment. We ask our clients to name the things they want and then we help them get those things.

As a coach, an arm-chair Buddhist and a modern seeker I stand at this juncture looking for the connection,

HOLLY MORRIS BENNET

groping for a way to reconcile these seemingly irreconcilable positions. The Buddha was quite clear that none of us should accept any doctrine without examining for ourselves and deciding in our own minds whether that doctrine leads to benefit and happiness.[18] This may be the thing I love most about Buddhism; it trusts, indeed requires, that each of us explore the ideas presented and decide for ourselves. And as I stand here wondering how these two roads I travel connect, I confront the fact that my experience is a square peg and this doctrine is a round hole. But when I peer through the window opened by my coaching experiences and look inside the sangha of two, I see the shapes shifting.

***

My client is sitting on the floor of her bedroom surrounded by magazines, scissors, tape, glue, pens, and glitter. We have done the future-self exercise and she has connected with the centered person inside her, the person she would be if she stopped listening to internal critics, naysayers, and seductive saboteurs. Using this radiant, happy energy, she is collaging a vision for her life.

We had talked about her goal of becoming a financial planner, but as she collages, the vision that emerges is all about "home." A panel full of desire blooms on the page. The house on Queen Anne Hill, the comfy chairs, the tea, the books, the quilts, and the children—all are there. As she speaks of her vision, she sounds happy, purposeful, focused, and alive. She has a hard time asking for the things she wants, but with this picture, she has found a voice for a deep longing. And I wonder how or if we're going to get to financial planner from here.

We remain in touch with each other after our coaching ends and she often refers back to this collage as the fuel for what she is up to. Before I go to New Zealand, I visit her. She has moved into a house with a new partner. It is as if the collage has come to life. Not long after this a wedding announcement, and then, finally the financial planner's license underway. I am happy for her and she tells me again, how useful she found it to create a vision for herself with the collage. When I scrutinize her desires and watch them at work in her life, I don't see suffering and I wonder about the Buddha's warnings.

***

My coach and I are talking about the novel I am writing. I think, at the time, this conversation is about completing the project, about finding a way to finish what I have started and worked so hard on. I tell him that my desire to see the book finished is so great, it almost hurts. It is painful to see over one hundred pages of creative effort foundering on my desk. I am very attached to this project. I have decided the book needs some research and I tell him I want to go on a road trip to do it. I want to get in my car and leave my life for ten days to drive through California, Nevada, and Arizona to find out the things I need to know to finish this novel.

As I talk, this desire takes a different shape. It becomes exciting, adventurous, and seductive; it resonates so perfectly with my primary value of freedom that it is like hearing Pavarotti hit an exquisite note. The vibrations are captivating! It is as if a different person is speaking now, and my coach notices the pain has given way and "she" has entered the room. It is my future self, the woman in me who has solitary adventures that transform her. She is not attached to this book. She is in love with me no matter what. To her the book is simply a way to expand me as a person and develop my spirit.

My coach sees this too. He pinpoints this desire and together we explore the idea of the road trip. As we do, he is tracing the line of my desire with me, treating it as if it were his own, loving it with that much energy, and always consciously keeping track of the thread so that if the sense of grasping comes back into the conversation, he can steer it toward something more productive or toward releasing it altogether. The idea of the trip dies, and he does nothing to resurrect it. Rather we now sit in the benefit that accrued from following the thread of my desire. It has opened up a book different from the one I am writing. The new book is the one where my life's journey is being written, and our following the road trip idea has awakened a different and deeper desire—to be the author of my own life. I revisit this interaction later with a specific question in mind: what was the effect of my desire? I see it produced some suffering in the beginning and I see how we transformed it inside my coaching sangha by using our process to follow it to a place of growth and understanding.

***

Looking again at the juncture between Buddhism and coaching I come to these conclusions. Desire is natural, powerful and an integral part of human nature. If we listen well enough, our desires can point us toward that life purpose that is uniquely ours. If we are courageous enough, they can propel the actions needed to manifest that unique life purpose in the world. Both my client and I have a stronger sense of our selves than we did before as a result of following the thread of our desires. Both of us needed to really own part of our selves, to satisfy certain needs, before we could continue certain aspects of our spiritual development. There are some desires, I think, that are fundamental to us as human beings (family, connection, home, self-respect) and ignoring them or pretending that we do not feel those needs is not spiritually productive.

Coaching, with its focus on life purpose, provides a beautiful entry point to access the question of desire and help people engage it without being burned by it. Aware coaches can help their clients recognize and work those fundamental cravings to develop the healthy self that precedes the experience of non-self. In this way we can *use* desire, rather than be used by it. Standing beside and facilitating another person's work with desire, possibly the most spiritually dangerous of all our perceptions, is a rare service. Wanting is human. Wanting as a way to enlightenment is transformative. This is the kind of work that needs two sets of eyes. It needs a sangha of two.

APPENDIX A
The Future Self Visualization

The following visualization is based on a future self exercise used in The Coaches Training Institute workshop. Feel free to use these exact words. Invite your client to get comfortable, perhaps lower the light level, make sure there will be no distractions, and play quiet, meditative music. When the client is grounded and ready, begin the visualization. Pause at appropriate times throughout the visualization to give the client sufficient time to be with the location or answer the questions. Allow a little time at the end for debriefing, but make the continued exploration of the visualization the homework for the upcoming week.

***

Get into a comfortable position. Now allow your eyes to close and begin by focusing your awareness on your breath. Breathing in and breathing out. Breathing in easily and effortlessly. Then breathing out. Each breath allows you to become more relaxed and comfortable. Outside sounds only allow you to go deeper inside: a reminder of how good it is to leave the noise and stress of the outside world and journey into the quiet and peace of your own inner world.

(Include the next paragraph only when you want the client to go to an even deeper meditative space.)

As you allow yourself to go deeper into a state of relaxation, perhaps you can remember a time when you stood before a pond or a lake and it was quiet and peaceful. You may have tossed a pebble into the center and noticed the ripples spreading out. One ripple after another, flowing outward, farther and farther. The ripples slowing down, becoming farther apart, until the water was once again calm and peaceful. I'm going to invite you now to imagine that your body is like that body of water. And as you drop a pebble into the center of your body, you can feel ripples of relaxation spreading out.

Waves of relaxation flowing through your body. Up through your torso into your chest and your back. Up through the vertebrae and spreading out into each and every muscle of your back. Through your shoulders and arms, up through your neck, your jaw, face, scalp. Feeling those ripples relax you as your muscles let go and become soft and loose. Feeling the ripples of relaxation flowing down the bottom of your torso. Flowing through your abdomen and your pelvis. Down through your thighs, calves, ankles, and toes. Know that each time you drop a pebble into the center of your body you can become more relaxed.

As you become more relaxed, you find yourself becoming

more quiet and peaceful. Now bring your attention to the spot between your eyes: the third eye. Imagine a light there. What color is the light between your eyes?

Now imagine that light becoming a beam that extends out into space. Follow that beam as it leaves this building, as it travels above the city, as it continues out, so that you can make out the entire area. Keep going further and further out into outer space and notice the curvature of the earth. As you keep going further and further out, you find yourself enveloped by the softness and quiet of space. Notice the big blue-green ball below you with the white clouds whisping around it. Allow yourself to enjoy this perspective for a moment.

Now notice another beam of light very near to you, a different color from the one you followed into outer space. Begin to follow that beam back down to earth. The beam is taking you back to earth twenty years from now, twenty years into the future. Keep following this beam down, noticing the curvature of the earth and the geography stretched out below you. As you come closer to the end of the beam, keep noticing where you are. This is where your future self lives, you, twenty years from now.

Come into contact with the earth and notice where you are. Notice what dwelling or nature surrounds you. Now move to the dwelling of your future self. What does it look like? What kind of landscape does it have? Are there trees? Flowers? What kind? Get a sense of this place.

Now get someone to come to the door. On the other side of the door is your future self waiting to greet you: yourself twenty years from now. As the door opens, what do you notice? Greet your future self and notice the way your future self returns your greeting, welcoming you into this time and place twenty years in the future. Take in this person—your future self. What does this person look like? Notice how this person stands, what this person is wearing. Get a sense of this person's essence. Notice the inside of this dwelling. What kind of person lives here? What are the colors of this place?

Now move with your future self to a comfortable place for a conversation. Perhaps your future self offers you something to drink. Settle in and make yourself comfortable for a talk with your future self. There are questions that you might want to ask your future self. Begin by asking:

"What is it, future self, that you most remember about the last twenty years?" Take a moment now to hear the answer. *(Pause.)* Now ask your future self the following question: "What do I need to know to get me from where I am now to where you are? What would be most helpful?" Listen to what your future self has to tell you. *(Pause.)* Good.

Now take a moment and ask your future self your own questions. What other questions would you like to ask your future self? *(Pause.)* And now ask your future self one final question before you go: "What name, other than your first name, are you called by? A special name. It could be a metaphor or a symbol of your essence. What is this name?" *(Pause.)* Good. Bringing this visit with your future self to a close, thank this person for being here with you today and sharing so much wisdom.

Now find your way back to the beam of light and journey back up the beam, watching this world twenty years in the future grow ever smaller as you move out into space. Again you see the ball of blue and green below you, clouds swirling around it. Notice that your beam of light has intersected with a different beam of light that will take you back to this year and this location. Follow this beam of light back to the present time on earth. As you travel down this beam, notice the earth growing bigger and bigger. Moving further down the beam, notice the geography of the area, the skyline and landscape of the area, and, finally, come back into the room here. Good. In a few moments I'm going to count from three to one. At the count of one, you will be refreshed and alert, as if you've had the perfect amount of rest, knowing you can remember everything you wish of this inner journey.

When you open your eyes, please remain silent and jot down things you want to remember about your journey. *Three.* Coming back to present time, becoming more alert and refreshed. *Two.* Stretching your body, feeling the ground beneath you. And *one.* Eyes open, refreshed and alert.

ENDNOTES

[1] Pāli is the liturgical language in which the doctrines of Buddhism (also known as the Pāli Canon) were written down in Sri Lanka in the 1st century b.c.e. Sanskrit, the classical language of India, is both liturgical and spoken. While recognizing there are many subtly different translations for the terms in this book, I have opted use the Sanskrit terms and simple English translations.

[2] Lama Surya Das, *Awakening the Buddha Within: Tibetan Wisdom for the Western World*, New York, NY: Broadway Books, 1998, p. 207.

[3] Ibid., p. 25.

[4] Ibid., p. 80.

[5] Ibid., pp.116-117.

[6] Ibid., pp. 121-122.

[7] Ibid.

[8] Sister Khema, "A Dhamma Talk Edited for *Bodhi Leaves*," http://www.accesstoinsight.org/lib/authors/khema/b1095. html.

[9] There are a few ways to access this part of the client. The "future self" visualization is reprinted in Appendix A. For some people, however, the visualization does not work well. One way to help a client develop a sense of the future self is through collage, having the client collect images that speak to her and then create a visual piece. Another way to access this part of a client is to pose the following question: What would you do with your time (not money) if you won the lottery? Describe a perfect day, a perfect week, a set of perfect months, and a perfect year.

[10] Lama Surya Das, *Awakening the Buddha Within,* p. 184.

[11] Ibid., p. 77.

[12] Ibid., pp. 76-89.

[13] Ibid., p. 84.

[14] This perspective on transition is well developed in the works of William Bridges and Gail Sheehy. Centerpoint Institute for LifeWork Renewal, Seattle, Washington, created the seasonal metaphor and has designed an extensive program

supporting people in transition based on this understanding of the cycle. More information on their programs is available at www.centerpointonline.org.

[15] See Elisabeth Kübler-Ross, M.D, *On Death and Dying: What the Dying have to Teach Doctors, Nurses, Clergy and Their Own Families,* New York, NY: Touchstone, 1969.

[16] The "Middle Way" refers to the path between materialism and aestheticism laid out by the Buddha. Here it is used in the generic sense, but with an acknowledgement of the Buddhist meaning.

[17] Lama Surya Das, *Awakening the Buddha Within,* p. 215.

[18] The *Kalama Sutra.*

Made in the USA